The Complementary Roots of Growth and Development

Taner Akan

The Complementary Roots of Growth and Development

Comparative Analysis of the United States, South Korea, and Turkey

palgrave
macmillan

Taner Akan
Department of Economics, Istanbul University
Istanbul, Turkey

Department of International Development
King's College London, London, UK

ISBN 978-3-319-68931-9   ISBN 978-3-319-68932-6   (eBook)
https://doi.org/10.1007/978-3-319-68932-6

Library of Congress Control Number: 2017955940

Cover pattern © Melisa Hasan

Printed on acid-free paper

This Palgrave Pivot imprint is published by Springer Nature
The registered company is Springer International Publishing AG
The registered company address is: Gewerbestrasse 11, 6330 Cham, Switzerland

About the Book

The common institutional roots of success and failure in economic growth and development (G&D) lie in the systemic governance and fragmentation of institutional complementarities, respectively, but not in the unilateral adaptation of market-led or state-led models. This book utilizes case countries such as the United States, South Korea, and Turkey—an advanced and developed, a newly developed, and a developing country, respectively—to adjudge how G&D succeeded or failed under market-led or state-led models. Akan provides a simple framework for understanding two points which go beyond ideological obsession. The first is how a model of G&D works and evolves, with its economic, financial, industrial, and political dynamics intertwining. The second is why a market-led or state-led model succeeds and fails in both developed and developing countries.

Contents

List of Abbreviations and Acronyms

AKP	Justice and Development Party of Turkey
BOK	Bank of Korea
CEA	Council of Economic Advisers
ERP	Economic Report of the President
FCIC	Financial Crisis Inquiry Commission
FED	Federal Reserve System
FEP	Full employment period
G&D	Growth and development
GDP	Gross domestic product
GRP	Great Recession Period
GSNP	Great Stagnation Period
GSP	Great Stagflation Period
IC	Institutional complementarity
IMF	International Monetary Fund
NIC	Negative institutional complementarity
NLP	Neoliberal period
NSTC	National Science and Technology Council
OECD	Organisation for Economic Co-operation and Development
OPEC	Organization of the Petroleum Exporting Countries
PE	Political economy
PIC	Positive institutional complementarity
PSBR	Public sector borrowing requirement
PTP	Priority Transformation Program

R&D   Research and development
SMEs   Small- and medium-sized enterprises
SOEs   State-owned enterprises
SPEC   Securities and Exchange Commission
TCMB   Turkish Central Bank
TKB   Turkish Ministry of Development
WTO   World Trade Organization

List of Figures

List of Tables

Introduction

Beyond a business cycle, the global political economy has been experiencing a paradigmatic crisis at both the theory and practice levels. The state-led and market-led models, the two potential alternatives for governing an economic system ended up, inter alia, with the Great Stagflation of the 1970s and the current Great Recession. For economic growth and development, henceforth referred to as G&D, this fact poses two challenges.

First, there is no definite alternative to the G&D strategy among the available choices both for the developed and developing countries. Developed countries such as the United States and South Korea, which adopted market-led and state-led models since the post-World War II (post-war) period, respectively, succeeded initially but failed (or had limited success) in achieving economic efficiency, improving social equity, and sustaining industrial progress.

The United States, as an advanced *market-led* model, achieved higher economic growth with lower-income inequality during the full employment period of 1948–1972 (FEP) than during the neoliberal period of 1980–2006 (NLP). During the NLP, the country's political economy fell into institutional fragmentation, culminating with the Great Recession of the last decade (Chap. 2).

South Korea achieved an economic miracle during the 1960s and 1970s when it adopted a *state-led model*. But then the country has failed in sustaining comparatively higher levels of growth and in improving social equity, though increasing the technological intensity of its exports during the transition to a *market-led* regime, particularly from the early 1990s onward (Chap. 3).

Developing countries like Turkey and Brazil adopted both models from the 1960s onward, but failed or achieved limited success in creating economic efficiency, improving social equity, and in unleashing innovation-driven industrial progress. For example, Turkey adopted a *state-led model* during the period 1960–1979 and then shifted to a *market-led model* from the early 1980s. The country failed to achieve the average growth of developing countries, in unleashing an innovation-driven G&D or in improving social equity (Chap. 4).

Second, the institutional matrix of a G&D process is presently much more complex, making it difficult to contrive a viable strategy. Besides the United States, many European, East Asian, and Latin American countries experienced catastrophic economic and financial crises during the NLP, as the outcome of institutional fragmentation (Streeck 2014; Wade 1998; Kingstone 2011). Apparently, these countries should modulate their fragmented structures assuming regulatory discretion to achieve competitive industrial transformation, comanage adverse consequences and beneficial opportunities of international trade, harness the destabilizing impact of external shocks, and so on. There are, however, both national and international impediments to achieving this.

The international trade and financial regime under the auspices of the World Trade Organization (WTO) and a flexible exchange rate system obviated the implementation of state-led or liberal protectionist strategies pursued by developed countries such as South Korea, Taiwan, and Italy during their takeoff periods in the 1960s and the 1970s. In the absence of a worldwide recession or depression until the early 1970s, economic systems evolved under a fixed-exchange rate regime, lower rate of international trade subject to protective measures, productivity-based competition, high growth paths, and abundant aggregate demand.

At the national level, given the potential risks, a government is restricted between adopting a unidirectional import-substitutionist and export-led growth strategy (Wilson 2012). The former would result, inter alia, in the granting of market monopolies to unviable enterprises in selected industries, in the accumulation of an unsustainable financial burden on the central budget and the depletion of foreign exchange reserves, a hike in interest rates, and the overvaluation of domestic currency (Lin 2009: 29–47). In contrast, export-led growth would result in exposing firms in the infant or strategic sectors to unfettered competition and exchange rate risks, thereby deterring investors in these sectors from taking entrepreneurial risks to set off innovation-driven progress, and so on.

Moreover, albeit designed impeccably, a G&D strategy may not be effective in a democratic system as incumbent governments typically, at best, strike a balance between their short-term and the country's long-term goals, which are in the grip of power competition between opposing parties, business circles, and labor organizations. Add to this transnational constraints such as limited potential for gaining competitive advantage in certain (especially, high-value-added) sectors that are dominated and monopolized by technologically advanced production centers, and political barriers to the implementation of extraterritorial components of G&D strategies due to regional or global distribution or clash of power.

The crisis of both state-led and market-led models and current challenges of selecting a G&D strategy pose not only practical challenges for policymakers but also theoretical challenges for academics attempting to explain the roots of institutional success and failure in G&D. In fact, an extensive research literature has examined these roots, adopting either neoclassical good governance or heterodox structuralist and institutionalist perspectives. These works range from Chang (2002) and Wade (1990) to Hall and Soskice (2001) and to Acemoğlu and Robinson (2012).

Against this background, this book aims to carve out the root causes of why a developing or a developed country, having adopted both state-led and market-led models, succeeds or fails in creating economic efficiency, improving social equity, and unleashing or sustaining innovation-driven industrial progress. For this purpose, it brings the above-noted complexities into the analysis to move beyond traditional state-centric or market-centric arguments. This book is based on the idea of carrying out an institutionalist analysis that neither favors neoliberal/interventionist models nor is drawn upon one-size-fits-all recipes such as those of good governance, because the explanation of failure and success in G&D using the monolithic assumptions of these models ends up in analytic deadlock. In particular, this book addresses questions such as the following:

How did South Korea and Taiwan achieve a developmental miracle despite the authoritarian rule in these countries in the 1960s and 1970s by adopting a state-led model that caused their then counterparts such as Turkey and Brazil, adopting democratic and authoritarian regimes in the same periods, respectively, to face drastic balance of account crises in the late 1970s?

How did the United States lead its competitors in the post-war period by adopting a market-led model that has since caused now-developing countries such as Turkey and Brazil, as well as other major Latin American countries, to perform considerably worse than in the 1960s and 1970s when they adopted inward-looking import substitutionism?

The analysis in this book draws on four main concepts: institutional complementarity (IC), systemic governance, institutional fragmentation, and the institutional trap. These four concepts taken together argue that (1) success and failure in G&D occur as a result of systemic governance and the fragmentation of ICs, respectively, and (2) enduring institutional fragmentation and drift between state-led and market-led strategies can create an institutional trap in G&D (see Chap. 1).

The following major components of a G&D process will be analyzed: economic policy, financial systems, corporate governance, industrial strategy, and political regimes. Specifically, the G&D strategies of the United States, South Korea, and Turkey are examined for two main reasons. The first is that they present three cases that experienced both success and failure or only failure under state-led or market-led models in different periods. The second is that they are advanced, developed, and developing market economies, respectively, having a per capita income of around $50,000, 30,000, and 10,000 dollars, respectively.

The approach of the presented analysis allows this book to make two novel contributions. The first is to explain the sources of institutional success and failure in G&D without subjecting our analysis to the monolithic assumptions of state-led or market-led models. The second is to demonstrate how state-led and market-led models in developed or developing countries might fail or succeed as a result of adopting a given mode of systemic governance or falling into institutional fragmentation and drift. These two analytical points are significant for showing that it is not the adoption of a state-led or market-led strategy per se but the systemic governance or fragmentation of the available institutions and factor endowments in time that underlies the success and failure of economic G&D in the long run.

The book has four chapters. The first chapter examines the roots of G&D success and failure in terms of systemic governance or the fragmentation of ICs. The second, third, and fourth chapters examine the success and failure of the United States, South Korea, and Turkey, respectively, using the analytic framework introduced in Chap. 1.

References

Acemoğlu, D., & Robinson, J. (2012). *Why Nations Fail: The Origins of Power, Prosperity, and Poverty*. New York: Crown Publishers.

Chang, H. (2002). *Kicking Away the Ladder: Development Strategy in Historical Perspective*. London: Anthem Press.

Hall, P., & Soskice, D. (2001). *Varieties of Capitalism: The Institutional Bases of Comparative Advantage*. Oxford: Oxford University Press.

Kingstone, P. (2011). *The Political Economy of Latin America: Reflections on Neoliberalism and Development*. London: Routledge.

Lin, J. Y. (2009). *Economic Development and Transition*. Cambridge: Cambridge University Press.

Streeck, W. (2014). *Buying Time: The Delayed Crisis of Democratic Capitalism*. London: Verso.

Wade, R. (1998). The Asian Debt-and-Development Crisis of 1997–?: Causes and Consequences. *World Development, 26*(8), 1535–1553.

Wade, R. (1990). *Governing the Market*. Princeton: Princeton University Press.

Wilson, G. (2012). Governance After the Crisis. In D. Levi-Faur (Ed.), *Oxford Handbook of Governance* (pp. 372–386). Oxford: Oxford University Press.

1

Systemic Governance and the Fragmentation of Institutional Complementarities

Abstract This chapter aims to explore the common institutional roots of success and failure in growth and development (G&D) for developed and developing countries. For this purpose, the chapter suggests an analytic frame that is drawn upon these four concepts of institutional analysis: complementarities, systemic governance, fragmentation, and trap. In doing so, the chapter concludes that the success and failure of G&D for both state-led and market-led models lie neither in liberalization nor in protection but in systemic governance and fragmentation of negative and positive complementarities, respectively. The following three chapters in the book will use the analytic frame suggested in this chapter to examine the success and failure of the United States, South Korea, and Turkey.

Keywords Complementarity • Growth • Development • Governance • Fragmentation • Trap

This chapter begins by defining ICs and their negative and positive dimensions. Then comes the definition of systemic governance and institutional fragmentation. The chapter ends with an explanation of the institutional trap.

1.1   Institutional Complementarity: Negative or Positive?

Institutional complementarity (IC) is used as an analytic concept principally in the literature of comparative political economy (PE) in order to explain the varieties of capitalism. In this literature, ICs are suggested to originate in the fact that the viability of an institutional form is strongly or entirely conditioned by the existence of several other institutional forms such that their conjunction offers better performance and greater resilience than alternative configurations (see Hall and Soskice 2001; Aoki 1994; Höpner 2005; Amable 2000: 659). In doing so, ICs generate two types of externalities. The first is *synergy*. For example, short-term finance, a corporate structure that concentrates authority in top management positions, and low-cost hiring and firing are, inter alia, three major ICs of the shareholder model of capitalism that is typically represented by the United States and United Kingdom. Top management in this model is thus able to adjust the labor demand of a firm according to changing market demands and operational costs. The second is *supplementarity* 'in which one institution makes up for the deficiencies of the others, such as the offsetting of the vicissitudes of a highly liberalized labor market through strong familial support' (Deeg 2007: 613: Crouch 2005).

ICs make sense essentially in the strategic convergence of a set of intersections for the realization of certain formal or informal aims. Thus, in systemic terms, the theory of intercomplementarity enables the analyst to shed light on the holistic equations of a PE regime. It is within this context that Boyer (2006: 57) defines intercomplementarity as 'one of the factors that provide the glue that holds together an overall institutional architecture'. Despite gaining strong impetus over the past two decades, however, there remains a systemic gap in the literature on ICs that precludes making a complementarity theoretic analysis of G&D from a systemic perspective. It relates to the fact that ICs are taken for granted as an exclusively positive phenomenon assuming that the existence of ICs always underlies better performance and greater resilience. For example, following Aoki (1994),

Hall and Soskice (2001: 17) argue that 'Two institutions can be said to be complementary if the presence (or efficiency) of one increases the returns from (or efficiency of) the other.' Underlying this is the positive connotation of the term *complementarity*, which is defined as 'relationship or situation in which two or more different things improve or emphasize each other's qualities' by the *Oxford English Dictionary*.

An exclusively positive delineation of ICs, however, bypasses negative ICs and hence turns out to be a partial rather than a systemic analysis. In G&D terms, the positive and negative here refer, respectively, to ICs that contribute to the formation and consolidation of economic efficiency, industrial sophistication and social equity or economic inefficiency, industrial leisure, and social inequity. Such a distinction does not mean that any institution can be suggested to generate a fully positive or fully negative influence from a functionalist perspective. Instead, the influence of each institution can be classified into one of these categories to varying degrees. What makes us classify its influence as negative or positive is the center of gravity of that influence on the systemic conduct of an institutional stock.

In this book, the following two suggestions are made to extend the scope of a complementarity theoretical analysis to an overall stock of developmental institutions. The first is that there are likely to be NICs in a PE structure that cause it to perform *worse* than alternative configurations. For example, the institutional systems of the Gulf countries are, inter alia, made up of four major NICs. The first is an authoritarian ruling strata financed through the incoming export revenues of primary commodities, fuel, and gas. The second is extensive and indiscriminate subsidies provided by the state to a leisure business class such as the free or below-cost provision of government services (utilities, transportation, sector-specific inputs) and low petroleum prices and subsidized long-term loans. The third is overvalued exchange rates due to the phenomenal current account and budgetary surpluses, causing the Dutch disease. And the fourth is social benefits and subsidies provided to public as the sources of regime justification such as extremely low level of direct or indirect taxes, housing, health, education, electricity, water, and fuel.

These four major NICs turn into a *negative synergy* prompting a positive-sum leisure among state, market, and society in these countries; sentence their economic development to low-value-added (petroleum related) primary products, such as rubber and plastic products, along with food and chemical goods; and, as a result, cause the region to be the least industrialized among the developing regions along with the sub-Saharan Africa (Askari 2006; UNDP 2011).

The second relates to the fact that NICs and PICs should be analyzed together to pin down how an institutional system works. It is not PICs or NICs per se but the overall clustering of both that determines how it works. For example, the state-led models of South Korea and Taiwan, during their developing or takeoff periods in roughly the 1960s and 1970s, essentially followed a PICs-dominated model. These PICs ranged from meritocratic, entrepreneurial forms of bureaucracy and well-functioning governance or deliberation councils between public and private sectors in managing industrial evolution to a gradual export-led industrial policy and patient money led by state banks for private investment in strategic, innovative and high-tech sectors, and so on. Beside these well-known PICs, both regimes included a number of NICs, too, such as the exclusion of pluralistic democracy, the suppression of organized labor, and the severe degradation of the environment (Wade 1990; Shin and Chang 2003).

These countries managed the evolutionary complications of their PICs and NICs using the former as a means of justifying the latter. Beyond any doubt, authoritarianism of any kind cannot be justified by any means. Because the people of these countries incurred unbearable costs of those NICs for a long period of time. In this sense, our point here is not that political authoritarianism would become a source of economic efficiency but that economic efficiency can be ensured under those authoritarian regimes that adopt a PICs-dominated systemic governance. These countries did so through *authoritarian entrepreneurship* as a mode of systemic governance, which mainly drew upon two managerial pillars. The first involved the authoritarian steering of production and distribution to establish workable mutuality between governmental development commitments and bureaucratic autonomy, protectionist liberalism and the innovative discretion of private enterprise, and political pressure and progressive wealth sharing. The second involved the optimization of developmental sequencing and timing between state entrepreneurial guidance and private enterprise-coordinated risk-taking and thus the prevention of unsustainable transformations or transaction costs to arise out of long-run institutional fragmentation and drift by means of consensual policy decisions made in well-functioning governance councils (Evans 1995; Ahrens 2002: 219–230).

Thus, with a slight revision that takes the above-described two points into consideration, ICs can be defined as *the mutual reinforcement of a certain group of institutions in part or all of a social structure that improves or worsens clustering relative to alternative configurations.* According to this definition, two points regarding a complementarity-based G&D analysis come to the fore. The first is that ICs can emerge as NICs and PICs. The second is that the potential impacts of ICs can affect a part or all of an institutional system. Thus, as noted by Boyer (2006: 55–56) and Deeg (2007: 615), ICs can be broken down into macro and micro components (please see Table 4.8 in Chap. 4).

1.2   Systemic Governance of Negative and Positive Complementarities

The definition of systemic governance requires first explaining what we understand from the terms *system* and *governance*. A *system*, in a social sense, denotes structures that have individual or organizational constituents interacting through value rationally or purposive rationally in shifting proportions and evolving intercomplementarily or interrepulsively over time and space.

In social theory, a systemic approach is used to explicate structures comprising a relatively large number of variables. This stems from the ever-increasing density and variety of cross-institutional interactions, as the number of actors, variables, interactions, concepts, and instances, along with the asymmetric structuration and destructuration of this institutional complexity, increases at the national or transnational levels with each cycle. In this sense, we should develop a *systemic* analysis of G&D governance because economic policy for development is at the crossroads of delicate balances and its structure and evolutionary dynamics can be understood only by incorporating all its basic components into a holistic analysis.

In developmental terms, governance can be defined, in broad strokes, as an institutionalized interaction between interdependent public and private actors for adjusting or monitoring a certain part or all of a developmental process under the guidance of predetermined rules and procedures. It is the decision-making, regulating, and monitoring roles of governance over both micro- and macroelements of an institutional stock that inspires us to analyze it from a systemic and complementarity perspective. To reveal the formational and evolutionary dynamics of a governance structure, an analyst should explain all its actors' value-rational or purposive-rational actions, the ever-increasing density and ever-changing variety of their interactions, and the multilateral implications of all major institutional intersections in an institutional environment.

I refer to *systemic governance* as a process of decision-making, regulation, and monitoring that aims to manage present and evolutionary complications of micro-macro NICs and PICs through the establishment of coherence and sustainability of an overall institutional stock. In G&D terms, the difference between systemic governance and major patterns of governance such as good governance, interactive governance (Torfing et al. 2012), democratic governance (Bevir 2010), or network governance (Jones et al. 1997) lies in two points.

The first relates to the fact that systemic governance serves not only as a mechanism of mutual enforcement to achieve standard or tailor-made positive externalities such as joint problem-solving, experimental learning, and policy know-how but also as a process of managing the coexistential and coevolutionary complications of NICs and PICs within the confines of endogenous factor endowment and institutional idiosyncrasies. As a result, the second point relates to the fact that unlike good governance, systemic governance is not necessarily geared toward mediating a certain model of G&D in the context of the private or public ordering of institutions but is geared toward governing the interplay between public and private actors in ensuring and sustaining the viability and coherence of an overall institutional stock for the effectuation of a G&D regime in either NICs-dominated or PICs-dominated structures.

Systemic governance may work with different combinations of efficiency or inefficiency, equity or inequity, and democracy or authoritarianism and in a PICs- or NICs-dominated manner. In this regard, in addition to South Korea and Taiwan, as shown in Table 1.1, among other examples of systemic governance (of PICs and NICs), we cite *productive solidarity* of Germany applied during the post-war period between democracy, efficiency, and equity (Streeck 1997); Italy's liberal protectionist regime of 1950–1973 between democracy, efficiency, and inequity (Grabas 2014); and the Gulf countries' *authoritarian leisure* between authoritarianism, inefficiency, and inequity. (The following discussion in this section on this topic only aims to provide an insight into systemic governance in general terms. In the following chapters, two cases of systemic governance, namely full employment in the United States between 1948 and 1972 and the authoritarian entrepreneurship of 1961–1979 in South Korea, are examined more in detail.)

The post-war German model drew upon a democratically structured systemic governance regime, *productive solidarity,* between efficiency, equity, and democracy. Between the end of World War II and unification, West German society engendered this model on the basis of an open economy and strong international competitiveness founded upon high wages, an extensive social welfare regime, and low-income inequality. The vertical fragmentation of the German state between the federal government and the *Länder* prevented it from pursuing an extensive and activist industrial policy with the exception of ad hoc interventions to control and address shortages in the areas of raw material extraction and transportation (Gruner 2014: 93).

Instead, the German state chose to politically institute the market structure by legally regulating micro- and macro-level industrial democracy through work councils and state-enabled neocorporatist councils, respectively. It also offered firms a range of infrastructural support such as high public spending on R&D. In a slightly liquidated market structure, the majority of investment came from banks in the form of long-run credit, typically cultivated from the savings of German workers. This

Table 1.1 Selected models of systemic governance in G&D

	Models and their approximate timespans	Democratic	Authoritarian	Efficiency	Equality	Dominated by
Germany	Productive solidarity, 1950s–1980s	+	–	+	Low	PICs
Italy	Liberal protectionism, 1950s to mid-1970s	+	–	+	High	PICs
South Korea and Taiwan	Autocratic entrepreneurship, 1960s and 1970s	–	+	+	Moderate	PICs
Gulf states	Authoritarian leisure, ongoing	–	+	–	High	NICs

enabled German firms to maintain decent labor standards such as high wages and investment in employee training and turn the market price into a means of quality competition through product specialization (Streeck 1997).

Another example of systemic governance was Italy's *liberal protectionist* development policy of 1950–1973. The adoption of liberal protectionism, as defined by Giuliano Amato, makes sense in a gradually liberalizing market economy such as the context of the Common Market in 1948–1968 as well as in an interventionist democratic state that emphasizes state holdings and enterprises, then the largest in the Western world, along with public direct investment.

The aims of the Italian state's activist industrial policy were twofold. The first goal was to promote economic growth, particularly in key strategic industries such as metallurgy, manufacturing, and chemicals, as well as to break up the then existing private monopolies in some sectors. The second was to alleviate income inequality, through the expropriation of private property if needed, as stipulated by the Italian constitution. In addition, the Italian state allowed itself license to invest in and finance key industries in the private sector through the gradual downsizing of trade restrictions and targeted incentives such as soft loans. Italy's average per capita growth of 4.9 percent in 1950–1973 was the second highest after West Germany (5 percent) among developed European countries, although the extent of social equity in the country remained questionable. As a result, in this period, Italy became an advanced industrial economy built on a more or less backward structure (Grabas 2014).

Contrary to these PICs-dominated regimes, Gulf countries effectuated a NICs-based systemic governance regime, *authoritarian leisure*, between inefficiency and inequity. Under such a regime, as noted above, the viability of the system was based on financing public and private productivity gaps through the export revenues of primary commodities and the prevention of social upheaval by offering patrimonial social subsidies.

The four models in Table 1.1 were selected to illustrate the major varieties of systemic governance as an institutional G&D strategy between efficiency, equity, authoritarianism, and democracy. In this sense, as shown in the table, all four models provide and sustain the viability and coherence of an institutional stock; however, they manage these stocks in different ways: (1) by using democratic or autocratic means of governance and (2) in a NICs- or PICs-dominated manner. Nevertheless, these divergences do not remove the systemic nature of these governance models because the main criterion for a model of developmental governance to be called systemic is not what means are used to manage it but whether the viability and coherence of an overall institutional stock are ensured between conflict, dependence, and order.

Systemic governance analysis draws on the various combinations of democracy, authoritarianism, efficiency, and equity for two reasons. The first is that the positive boundedness of a developmental governance analysis in the sense of preconditioning the existence of a PICs-dominated regime makes three things impossible: (1) considering the inefficiency- and inequity-creating NICs of an institutional system, (2) jointly analyzing the unfolding NICs and PICs, and (3) providing a process-based discussion on how a NICs-dominated systemic governance regime can evolve into a PICs-dominated one.

The second is, in a similar vein, that to confine the scope of governance only to democratically mediated interactions causes another positive boundedness. This prompts the exclusion of the anti-democratic processes of interaction and fails to explain the interlaced evolution of democracy and authoritarianism or the path-dependent change from authoritarian to democratic structures from a governance theoretic perspective.

Governance, in developmental terms, 'refers to the modes and manner of governing' (Jessop 1998: 30). And what makes governance democratic or authoritarian is the equal or unequal division of power among participant actors (equal power sharing in the stages of decision-making, enforcement, and cost- or benefit-sharing are suggested to ensure input, throughout, and output legitimacy, respectively [Scharpf 1999]). In this sense, the mere existence of plurality in metagovernance councils in governing one or each of these stages does not automatically bring about democracy (Jessop 1998: 19–20). Indeed, the participant actors of governance act under the shadow of hierarchy and the principal, state, can retract the delegation made (Torfing et al. 2012: 41–42). In this case, the formal existence of governance institutions loses its democratic meaning. From this emerges an *autocratic governance* under changing levels of inequality of power among participants, as was the case in South Korea and Taiwan.

1.3 Institutional Fragmentation and Drift

Does every country have a systemic governance regime? If not, what outcomes does its absence cause? Answering these questions entails understanding three interdependent elements. The first is a decision-making body such as metagovernance structures, a democratic or authoritarian state, or bureaucratic apparatus that has the managerial capacity to steer or provide coherence to an institutional stock; second, the available stock of political, economic, and cultural institutions; and finally, actors that mediate institutional interactions through democratic or authoritarian governance mechanisms.

Without the first element, the systemic coordination of the available institutions cannot be ensured. Indeed, the structure or quality of the available institutions and mediating actors' strategies determine the operational scope of the first element. However, the first element cannot enforce its steering or commanding function properly if the latter two do not offer intercomplementary feedback. For example, what made the miracle of autocratic entrepreneurship possible in South Korea was not only the existence of well-functioning metagovernance institutions or the bureaucratic strata's genius of industrial management. Equally important were the entrepreneurial, innovative, and export-expansive strategies of private sector enterprises (*chaebols*), particularly in high-tech industries, as well as the large educational investment of households (Short 1984: 119–120; Mee and Park 2011).

Each country, in this regard, may not have these three peculiarities simultaneously. Out of the absence of a systemic governance arises an *institutional fragmentation* which refers to the lack of an intercomplementary linkage between decision-making structures, available formal-informal institutions, and the strategies of mediating actors. As an analytic concept, institutional fragmentation denotes that a country's G&D strategy fails or achieves limited success mainly as a result that this country has been unable to orchestrate its own proper ICs under a mode of systemic governance, but instead manages its developmental institutions through either ad hoc or transposed strategies.

As a result, in the case of institutional fragmentation, unilateral design by a democratic or authoritarian state per se that does not have the necessary power or discretion to steer or command the other two elements or rules in the absence of a competitive and innovative private sector cannot be expected to harness the destabilizing and efficiency-reducing impact of this fragmentation. This is what many developed or developing countries such as South Korea and Turkey have experienced roughly over the last four decades (see Chaps. 3 and 4). In a similar vein, an unregulated market structure cannot be expected to eliminate the same negative impact, too, in the absence of a state-coordinated systemic governance. In this sense, as to be detailed in Chap. 2, the Great Depression of 1929 and the Great Recession of today in the United States have also emanated from a process of institutional fragmentation in the grip of unregulated market structures.

It is untenable in both the cases to ensure the viability and consistence of an overall institutional stock in the long run (see Goodin 1996: 30–34). Instead, the design-centered policy choices on the basis of transposed ideas or the uncontrolled deregulation of financial and commercial markets in both developed and developing cases have prompted an enduring *institutional drift*, the runaway and unplanned flow of the NICs and PICs. This drift emanates from asymmetric adjustments between two rash assumptions. The first is that the enduring practical challenges of making G&D more efficient or more equal can be eliminated by a state-led unilateral design or by a market-led spontaneous action. The second is that design-centered restructurations or uncontrolled deregulations might be implemented in a short period of time regardless of the proper alignment of local NICs and PICs.

At this stage, another point should be clarified: if systemic governance might occur in a NICs-dominated structure, then how can we distinguish a NICs-dominated *fragmented* mode of governance from a NICs-dominated *systemic* mode of governance? The latter is made possible by the coordination of NICs that effectuates an ordered mode such as the corporatist welfarism seen in Gulf countries. Despite the lack of systemic coordination in the former mode, NICs continue to complement each other but in a fragmented manner. In other words, under both the systemic and the fragmented modes of governance, NICs continue to generate inefficiency, inequity, or industrial leisure. What distinguishes the latter from the former is that NICs drift rather than being managed by an authority or metagovernance institution.

Finally, institutional fragmentation is not only an issue of liberalization/deregulation or network failure. It differs from liberalization in the sense that its mainstay is not the evolution of a country's ICs under a market-dominated structure but the lack of a systemic governance regime to manage the present and evolutionary complications of a country's ICs. In other words, as will be discussed with reference to the United States, South Korea, and Turkey in the following chapters, institutional fragmentation can cause inefficiency and inequity in both state-led and market-led models. Moreover, it encompasses not only the networks of production but also those of politics, economics, and culture. Thus, the root cause of institutional fragmentation is not the disjunction of production-related networks but the lack of an intercomplementary dynamic between formal/informal institutions and the strategies of major economic and political actors.

1.4   Institutional Trap or Income Trap?

The long-run fragmentation and drift of a country's NICs and PICs evolve into an institutional trap, which can be defined as a specific stage in which a country is unable to formulate or implement a model of systemic governance to transform a NICs-dominated G&D structure into a PICs-dominated one. Thus, in the case of an institutional trap, policymakers become stuck between the requirement of making structural or systemic changes and the path dependencies of enduring institutional fragmentation.

The institutional trap differs from the middle-income trap in three main ways: (1) it can occur in developing as well as developed countries, (2) it develops in the long term rather than from short-term G&D experiences, and (3) it arises out of the interlocking of political, economic, and cultural institutions in a NICs-dominated structure rather than the mere inability of a country to increase its GDP per capita above a certain threshold.

For example, as elaborated on in Chap. 2, the United States faces an institutional trap between low growth, high inequality, and industrial leisure, and the country's policymakers do not have a clear plan for leaving this trap because the set of policy choices and their potential consequences are complicated and ambiguous. In particular, these challenges facing the US economy have accumulated over four or five decades throughout a process of fragmentation and cannot be deaccumulated by *conjuncturally countercyclical* policy adaptations such as monetary easing. What is needed is *structurally countercyclical* change ranging from taxation to business ethics and the establishment of a workable, even if not absolute, trade-off among efficiency, equity, and democracy, as was the case during the full employment period (FEP) of 1948–1972 (see Chap. 2).

The Obama administration did not initiate structural change apart from imposing palliative regulatory constraints on the finance sector with the Dodd-Frank Act of 2010. The performance of the US economy during the Great Recession of 2007–2017 illustrates that nonsystemic policy changes, as opposed to improving efficiency and productivity, have further increased inequality in the country. The fact that the Trump administration is pushing hard to undo even the palliative regulations of the Dodd-Frank Act proves the embeddedness of the country's NICs-dominated structure.

1.5   Conclusion

Overall, there are three stages of an IC-theoretic developmental analysis in systemic governance terms. At the first stage, the PICs and NICs of a developmental structure are brought into analysis together to determine how this structure works in time. At the second stage, it is examined whether these NICs and PICs are managed through a systemic governance regime or they drift apart in an institutional fragmentation. At the third stage, possible venues may be found to erect or consolidate PICs-dominated structures in time. And this preconditions the establishment of a systemic governance regime to ensure the coherence and viability of an institutional stock, thereby preventing the genesis and embedding of institutional fragmentation. What should be emphasized is that the analytical key to G&D governance lies not in identifying standard or one-size-fits-all principles but in principles that would prove both workable and accessible in a specific context and that, unlike good governance, systemic governance of ICs serves as a facilitator of this purpose rather than as an ideal end in itself.

In the following, taking the cases of the United States, South Korea, and Turkey, the book focuses on the first two stages and brings in the third stage to discuss whether a strategy of structural transformation can succeed without considering the systemic and evolutionary complications of NICs and PICs.

References

Ahrens, J. (2002). *Governance and Economic Development: A Comparative Institutional Approach*. Cheltenham: Edward Elgar.

Amable, B. (2000). Institutional Complementarity and Diversity of Social Systems of Innovation and Production. *Review of International Political Economy, 7*(4), 645–687.

Aoki, M. (1994). The Contingent Governance Teams: Analysis of Institutional Complementarity. *International Economic Review, 35*(3), 657–676.

Askari, H. (2006). *Middle East Oil Exporters: What Happened to Economic Development?* Cheltenham: Edward Elgar.

Bevir, M. (2010). *Democratic Governance*. Princeton: Princeton University Press.

Boyer, R. (2006). How Do Institutions Cohere and Change?: The Institutional Complementarity Hypothesis and Its Extension. In P. James & G. Wood (Eds.), *Institutions, Production and Working Life* (pp. 13–61). Oxford: Oxford University Press.

Crouch, C. (2005). Complementarity and Fit in the Study of Comparative Capitalisms. In G. Morgan, R. Whitley, & E. Moen (Eds.), *Changing Capitalisms: Internationalization, Institutional Change, and Systems of Economic Organization* (pp. 167–189). Oxford: Oxford University Press.

Deeg, R. (2007). Complementarity and Institutional Change in Capitalist Systems. *Journal of European Public Policy, 14*(4), 611–630.

Evans, P. (1995). *Embedded Autonomy: States and Industrial Transformation.* Princeton: Princeton University Press.

Goodin, R. E. (1996). Institutions and Their Design. In R. E. Goodin (Ed.), *The Theory of Institutional Design* (pp. 1–54). Cambridge: Cambridge University Press.

Grabas, C. (2014). Planning the Economic Miracle? Industrial Policy in Italy between Boom and Crisis, 1950–75. In C. Grabas & A. Nützenadel (Eds.), *Industrial Policy in Europe After 1945* (pp. 134–161). New York: Palgrave.

Gruner, S. (2014). Ensuring Economic Growth and Socioeconomic Stabilization: Industrial Policy in West Germany, 1950–75. In C. Grabas & A. Nützenadel (Eds.), *Industrial Policy in Europe After 1945* (pp. 86–112). New York: Palgrave.

Hall, P., & Soskice, D. (2001). *Varieties of Capitalism: The institutional Bases of Comparative Advantage.* Oxford: Oxford University Press.

Höpner, M. (2005). What Connects Industrial Relations and Corporate Governance? Explaining Institutional Complementarity. *Socio-Economic Review, 3*(2), 331–350.

Jessop, B. (1998). The Rise of Governance and the Risks of Failure: The Case of Economic Development. *International Social Science Journal, 155,* 29–45.

Jones, C., Hesterly, W. S., & Borgatti, S. P. (1997). A General Theory of Network Governance: Exchange Conditions and Social Mechanisms. *The Academy of Management Review, 22*(4), 911–945.

Mee, E. K., & Park, G. K. (2011). The *Chaebol.* In B. Kim & E. F. Vogel (Eds.), *The Park Chung Hee Era: The Transformation of South Korea* (pp. 265–294). Cambridge, MA: Harvard University Press.

Scharpf, F. W. (1999). *Governing in Europe.* Oxford: Oxford University Press.

Shin, J., & Chang, H. (2003). *Restructuring Korea Inc.* London: Routledge.

Short, R. (1984). The Role of Public Enterprises: An International Statistical Comparison. In R. Floyd, C. Gary, & R. Short (Eds.), *Public Enterprises in Mixed Economies: Some Macroeconomic Aspects* (pp. 110–195). Washington, DC: International Monetary Fund.

Streeck, W. (1997). German Capitalism: Does It Exist? Can It Survive? *New Political Economy, 2*(2), 237–256.

Torfing, J., Peters, B. G., Pierre, J., & Sorensen, E. (2012). *Interactive Governance: Advancing the Paradigm.* Oxford: Oxford University Press.

United Nations Development Programme (UNDP). (2011). *Arab Development Challenges Report 2011: Towards the Developmental State in the Arab Region.* Cairo: UNDP.

Wade, R. (1990). *Governing the Market.* Princeton: Princeton University Press.

2

Rise and Fall of the Market-Led Model: The United States

Abstract Using the analytic frame suggested in Chap. 1, this chapter makes a comparative analysis of the American economic growth under four subsequent periods. These periods are the full employment of 1948–1972, the great stagflation of 1973–1979, the neoliberal period of 1980–2006, and the period of 2007–2017 that covers the great recession of 2007–2009 and the great stagnation of 2010–2017. The chapter examines the full employment regime as a systemic governance of American kind, the great stagflation as a period of initial institutional fragmentation, the neoliberal period as the embedding of this institutional fragmentation, and finally the period of 2007–2017 as a stage of institutional trap. The aim of the chapter is to illustrate how a market-led model might both succeed and fail, respectively, through the systemic governance and fragmentation of its positive and negative institutional complementarities.

Keywords United States • Growth • Institutions • Complementarity • Governance • Trap

© The Author(s) 2018
T. Akan, *The Complementary Roots of Growth and Development*,
https://doi.org/10.1007/978-3-319-68932-6_2

2.1   Introduction

The United States, by adopting a market-led model, achieved higher economic growth and lower income inequality during the FEP (1948–1972) than in the NLP between 1980 and 2006. The country's full employment strategy as a type of systemic governance became fragmented during the Great Stagflation Period (GSP) of 1973–1979. In the NLP, this fragmentation became embedded in a drifty process, ending up with low growth, high unemployment, and slackening industrial performance in the period of 2007–2017 that covers two sub-periods: the Great Recession Period (GRP) of 2007–2009 and the Great Stagnation Period (GSNP) of 2010–2017. In this chapter, the country's success and failure in these four periods are examined from a complementary theoretic perspective to illustrate what a market-led model might achieve through the systemic governance and fragmentation of its ICs.

The periodization of the American G&D in this chapter is flexible. The FEP may have also started from the New Deal of 1933–1939 or immediately after the end of World War II. I chose the year 1948 as the beginning of the FEP since the country's economic indicators became relatively stable with the declining influence of the war. Another reason is that the FEP as a mode of systemic governance became crystallized after World War II. Likewise, the GSP could also have started in 1970 or 1974. I chose the year 1973 because the high productivity of the 1960s continued until 1972 (Gordon 2012), when inflation increased by around 90 percent and began a steady upward trend; the (first) OPEC crisis also started in that year.

The symbolic year 1980 saw the birth of neoliberalism globally. The NLP might, however, have started with the Carter administration of 1977–1981 that enforced extensive industrial deregulations. Further, the key indicators of stagflation, unemployment with inflation, continued into 1982 when inflation began to fall.

This chapter has four sections. In the first section, US economic G&D is outlined from a complementary theoretic perspective. The second section examines the laissez-faire period as well as the FEP, GSP, and NLP with reference to economic policy and financial and corporate governance. In the third section, the influence of industrial and political governance on the country's G&D performance is examined. The chapter concludes by investigating the GRP and the GSNP as two sub-periods of institutional trap between 2007 and 2017.

2.2   A Complementary Theoretic Account of the American Growth

This section provides an inductive understanding of how a G&D system works in terms of the complementary linkages of governance structures. The qualitative and quantitative data underlying this section are drawn from the detailed elaborations in the subsequent sections.

The Root Cause: Laissez-faire

The laissez-faire mode of governance in the United States before the Great Depression was founded upon a finance-driven regime of investment and production in an unregulated setting with the infrequent supervision of banks' balance sheets, a self-regulated securities market, and stock exchanges that acted as cartels free from any legislation. The increasing speculation as well as the Fed's failure to take a proactive regulatory initiative and adjust the money supply resulted in the stock market crash of October 1929.

In this sense, one of the major negative institutional complementarities (NICs) in that period for the US economy was an unregulated financial market structure that had become a bubble over productive relations and hence sparked system-wide risks. Another NIC was the Fed's belief that monetary policy did not matter and that proactive regulation could unnecessarily cause economic contraction. These two NICs reemerged in the NLP and created, this time, the Great Recession.

The Full Employment as a Mode of Systemic Governance

Compared with the NLP, the PICs-dominated regime founded in the FEP was driven by the trade-off between higher growth and lower inequity along with a higher total factor and labor productivity in industrial sectors. In this period, policymakers tailored countercyclical rationality to harness the remnants of the laissez-faire period, generating a systemic governance of American kind whose positive institutional complementarities (PICs) are elaborated on below.

In the FEP, the existence of a stable presidential regime, two-level executive coordination, and an electoral system was used by policymakers to jointly regulate economic, financial, corporate, and industrial relations governance to ensure the sustainability of a growth-driven structure and the relative trade-off between efficiency and equity. The regulated clustering of these subsystems aggregated into full employment as a mode of systemic governance. This high and stable growth, employment, and relative income equality provided legitimacy to the US government in the eyes of both the market and broader society.

The fiscal policy during the FEP raised output and employment first by taking discretionary activism through high public investment and second by stimulating private consumption and investment with its (positive) multiplier impact. The accommodative monetary policy in the FEP focused on managing bank credit from a growth-driven perspective in line with the real bills doctrine and keeping interest rates at optimal levels so as not to reduce the marginal propensity to invest in nonfinancial markets. In addition to economic policy, an active industrial policy in an antitrust regulatory setting used such policy tools as basic research support, government subsidies, and tax exemptions, thereby complementing innovative R&D in the private sector. The resulting high private sector expenditure and employment along with higher total factor productivity yielded higher tax revenues and moderate budget deficits (in a low inflation setting until the late 1960s), thereby feeding back into the durability of discretionary and accommodative activism as well as the active industrial policy.

The state's regulatory activism in both the financial and the nonfinancial sectors in the FEP resulted in a trade-off between their profitability in the 1960s. This prevented the former from using the profits of the latter as a source of speculation and from growing in an uncontrolled manner by using excessive leverage. It also prevented the latter from developing imperfect competition in structural terms through antitrust laws. Thus, besides blocking a system-wide crisis, financial and industrial regulation also ensured the durability of innovative investment and the funding of this investment by issuing equities whose turnover rates were a couple of years and bank credit (but not by junk bonds).

Regulatory activism also led to better working conditions in the private sector by ensuring the durability of corporate governance, the legal basis for workers to get organized and have secure employment, as well as the protection of ordinary customers from high-risk financial investment. This higher productivity, output, and employment in the institutional setting of discretionary activism in the public sector and productivity-based corporate governance under a Fordist mode of production regime complemented regulatory activism by becoming positive indicators for its maintenance until the early 1970s when an anti-regulatory bias became salient.

The managerial mode of corporate governance by individual owners and managers in a mass production setting also increased output and employment through a competition strategy based on factor productivity and investment in patient capital. It also complemented the relatively low income inequality both by paying decent wages to employees in line with their productivity and by tying executive compensation to productivity rather than share prices. The consequent higher rates of household savings and consumer demand increased private sector investment, yielding higher tax revenues from the public sector to conduct selective and targeted industrial programs, particularly for small and startup firms, to foster competitive innovation in the marketplace.

In addition to the above-noted PICs, three main NICs occurred during the FEP. The first was an inflationary setting arising, inter alia, from the expansionary economic policy of the late 1960s, which had a relatively high rate of federal debt as a percentage of GDP. This became an underlying driver behind the fragmentation of the full employment regime in the early 1970s when combined with the skyrocketing oil prices during the OPEC crisis.

The second NIC was the lack of a tradition of dynamic governance between government and business as well as the absence of interfirm cooperation in steering industrial and sectoral development. Although not a systemic loophole during the FEP when there was abundant aggregate demand, the presence of antitrust regulations preventing massive industrial concentration and the threat of competition from the outside world resulted in this NIC feeding back into the erratic evolution and declining performance of the country's industrial sectors during the NLP.

The third NIC was the lack of a strong tradition of economic and industrial democracy that would otherwise both moderate the inflationary impact of the positive output gap and prevent the financialization of US economic governance in a turbulent manner, thereby mitigating system-wide shocks (this NIC led workers to incur tremendous declines in their incomes in the NLP, a key cause of plummeting household savings and consumer demand).

The Beginning and Embedding of Institutional Fragmentation

These three NICs did not overwhelm the PICs-dominated structure of the FEP until the beginning of the GSP. During the GSP, the major PICs of the FEP became detached from declining growth, rising inflation and unemployment, and soaring budget deficits. In the early 1970s, there emerged a wave of deregulation in major sectors. Government expenditure declined considerably, and the Fed adopted monetary aggregates targeting as its basic macroeconomic strategy in 1970. Thus, the institutional fragmentation of the full employment model started during the GSP. The hallmark of this fragmentation was that policymakers developed a reactive rationality to the public sector's discretionary activism and regulatory discretion in the grip of the pressure of deregulatory demands from the large corporations that embarked upon massive lobbying activities in the early 1970s.

In the NLP, the institutional fragmentation that had already started in the GSP became embedded, and it evolved in a drifty process of economic inefficiency, social inequity, and industrial leisure. (Industrial leisure refers to the trend in the entire period but does not deny the rising total factor productivity in the country between 1996 and 2004 during the third industrial revolution; see Gordon 2012.)

During the NLP, political governance focused on sustaining incumbency by engaging in rent-seeking action with financial and nonfinancial corporations both centrally and locally, thereby institutionalizing a deregulated economic, financial, and corporate governance. This deregulation was so embedded that the Democrat Party could not initiate systemically countercyclical actions despite taking some palliative measures, even during and after the housing bubble. By contrast, both Republicans and Democrats perpetuated their popularity with a pro-market rhetoric, becoming eligible for campaign finance as well as for the donations and votes of the rich whose electoral participation was higher than that of the poor.

System-wide fragmentation manifested itself in economic policy as a supply-side strategy. Specifically, consolidation-obsessive fiscal policy lowered aggregate demand not only through government expenditure, which was less than half that in the FEP, but also through its negative multiplier impact on private consumption and investment. The consequent lower growth, employment, and income equality caused lower tax revenues, higher budget deficits, and a public indebtedness on a par with that in the FEP, thereby feeding back into the durability of nondiscretionary fiscal policy.

An inflation-obsessive monetary policy with a rationality of post hoc interventionism failed to reduce inflation, manage the money supply and interest rates, and control asset prices; however, it contributed to financialization by failing to implement balance sheet regulation, to control credit expansion, to impose optimal reserve requirements on banks, and to prevent speculation by instruments such as stock margin requirements. In addition, when combined with such monetary policy, the lack of growth-driven regulatory discretion in financial governance promoted excessive leverage, asset price bubbles, the excessive complexity of the financial system, and the breakdown in accountability and ethics through legal arrangements such as those deregulating the asset-backed securities market and incentivizing the originators and investors of these securities.

Thus, both inflation-obsessive monetary policy and deregulated financial governance stimulated the financialization of the US economy. Indeed, the rising profitability and size of speculative financial investment compared with nonfinancial investment, particularly from the early 1990s until the housing bubble, helped maintain such unconstrained financial governance.

Financialization in the deregulated securities and product markets has led to three main outcomes. It has first focused the finance sector on originating and distributing high-risk financial derivatives, thereby stimulating volatility across the economic system. Second, it has driven corporate governance toward a shareholder focus with skyrocketing market capitalization, stock market prices, and earnings as well as the increasing size, speculative structure, and yields of the corporate bond market. Finally, it has reduced marginal propensity to invest in the nonfinancial sector, particularly between the early 1990s and the housing bubble when profitability compared with the financial sector declined remarkably (Palley 2013). These three causes jointly led a systemic crisis owing to an upsurge in indebtedness and the erosion of savings and aggregate demand; the increasing propensity of corporate governance to concentrate on short-term financial gains rather than on productivity; and hence the plummeting of the manufacturing sector's contribution to GDP.

In a shareholder model of governance, firms are managed by their institutional shareholders such as pension funds, mutual funds, insurance funds, and foreign investors, which are primarily interested in increasing equity value rather than long-run productivity. This model is also aligned with executive compensation tied to share prices, rampant market capitalization, weak risk management, and hostile takeovers. In addition, in deregulated labor markets, the shareholder model worsens income inequality and working conditions by widening the gap between real wages and labor productivity, lengthening working hours, lowering wages and job security, increasing labor turnover with easy hiring and firing rules, generating a highly segmented labor market between high- and low-skilled workers, and diminishing the quality of occupational training. Thus, the shareholder model resulted in lower private investment, household savings, and total factor and labor productivity along with higher income inequality and indebtedness and massive bankruptcies in the nonfinancial sector.

The deregulation of many key industries from the 1970s ended up with widespread industry concentration, the increase of rents accruing to a few firms, and a reduction in firm entry and labor market mobility, not to mention weak coordination among government, business, and organized labor in managing sectoral evolution, productivity gaps, and skill mismatches between sectors. As a result, the country lost its high-tech innovative power in the face of rising competition from Asian countries and its huge trade deficits. What aggravated declining industrial performance was mediocre educational quality in basic skills such as mathematics, reading, and science and the poor development of effective vocational and job training programs despite rising educational expenditure.

As a result, an economic policy obsessed with consolidation and inflation targeting, over-financialized economic governance, deregulated financial and corporate governance, and weak coordination and commitment among economic actors contributed to declining efficiency, equity, and industrial progress. In summary, financialization and deregulation in the NLP replaced full employment and regulation in the FEP. All these NICs evolved through a process of institutional fragmentation and drift rather than being managed by any mode of systemic governance. The result has been an enduring institutional trap during the Great Recession of 2007–2009 and the Great Stagnation of 2010–2017.

At first glance, the above delineation of US growth during the NLP might seem an utterly pessimistic account omitting the PICs in this era. Indeed, it could be said that industrial innovation and sophistication created competitive rigor, particularly in ICT and computer technologies. However, as will be elaborated in due course, in terms of *overall* manufacturing performance, the country's accomplishments exclusively in these two sectors cannot be accepted as a PIC that underlies overall industrial efficiency.

The Institutional Trap: Great Recession of 2007–2009 and the Great Stagnation of 2010–2017

During the GRP and the GSNP, the government and the Fed embarked on harnessing the immediate externalities of the NLP, which caused the housing bubble, rather than turning its NICs into PICs by launching systemic change similar to that initiated after the Great Depression. The government first adopted an expansionary policy in 2007–2009 and then turned to austerity in 2010 in the face of the highest average budget deficits of the past seven decades. The Fed also expanded its balance sheet more than fivefold between 2007 and 2017 by buying massive treasury securities and implementing quantitative easing until 2014 before reaching deadlock between reducing its balance sheet and fostering growth. In the grip of the (negative) multiplier impact of rising austerity, the business sector both increased its savings and returned its earnings to shareholders instead of using them for reinvestment. Further, the country's declining manufacturing performance and total factor productivity did not alleviate the pressure on fiscal policy but rather contributed to deepening the unfolding trap. Furthermore, during the GRP and the GSNP, income inequality increased and the gap between real wages and labor productivity widened remarkably.

Overall, the country's grim performance on investment, growth, and employment in the GRP, with a substantial increase in overall indebtedness, demonstrates that the poor recovery indicators are far from unleashing a durable high growth and low unemployment period. In other words, the country's institutional trap between low growth, high inequality, and slackening industrial performance seems to be continuing with the failure to reform the embedded NICs-dominated structure into a PICs-dominated one. The next decade is bound to unfold under the pressure of revising and reforming the country's flawed institutional stock.

2.3   Before the Great Depression of 1929

The laissez-faire years before the Great Depression of 1929 can be featured as a period when a NICs-dominated structure of the US economy between the state, market, and households became established and was the underlying cause of the Great Depression of 1929. The FEP was drawn upon transforming this structure into a PICs-dominated one. However, a similar set of NICs first re-emerged in the GSP and became re-established during the NLP, and finally underlying the GRP. As a result, the understanding of those NICs that sprouted off during the laissez-faire period is of significance in explaining the evolution of the country's political economy (PE) around World War II onward.

The laissez-faire capitalism of the early twentieth century was drawn upon a government that kept unions at bay, targeted a stable money supply, imposed trade barriers, and protected corporations from liability. Thus, laissez-faire in the country prevailed mainly in macroeconomic governance, financial governance, and corporate governance, which are examined in the following sections. In industrial governance, the US state had embarked on protecting new manufacturing giants, which will be examined under a separate section below.

The key NICs of this period that reemerged in the 1970s were, inter alia, an unregulated financial system and a finance-driven production regime. These NICs subjected savings-finance-investment intercourse into the fragmentizing impact of financialization, culminating in the most devastating crisis of the twentieth century, the Great Depression (financialization can be defined as 'the increasing dominance of the finance industry in the sum total of economic activity of financial controllers in the management of corporations of financial assets among total assets, of marketed securities, and particularly of equities, among financial assets, of the stock market as a market for corporate control in determining corporate strategies, and of fluctuations in the stock market as a determinant of business cycles' [Dore 2002: 116–117]). In terms of G&D, financialization is a process during which the role of the financial sector evolves from funding the nonfinancial sector to using the latter as a means to potentially cultivate funds for speculation.

In the United States, the securities market, particularly the formal stock exchanges, practiced self-regulation during the period 1801–1832. In case the states had passed an occasional law against market interests during a crisis period, they were mostly ignored. Banks were chartered by the Bank of the United States, the only national bank at that time. With the federal government withdrawing from banking regulation in 1836, many states required banks only a minimum amount of capital to commence their activities. After the federal regulation was reintroduced in the early 1860s, state-level regulation remained, resulting in a bifurcated system that enabled banks to choose a national- or state-level charter. What consolidated this model was the ineffective and infrequent examination of banks, apart from the exception of branching restrictions on banks (Vitols 2001).

In this model, banks evolved into proper financial institutions. Underlying this was the National Bank Act of 1863 that required national banks to buy treasury bonds and pledge them as collateral for the uniform national bank notes that they issued, causing the accumulation of large inventories of funds with New York bankers. As there was no discount market for bills of exchange, banks turned to the stock market and the call loan market for liquid assets. This enabled New York bankers to capitalize the savings of ordinary US households as a major source of leverage. And the rapid development and incorporation of the US industry facilitated this process. In 1869, the value added of the agriculture and manufacturing sectors was 53 percent and 33 percent, respectively. Within three decades, the same rates turned into 33 percent and 53 percent, respectively. The United States, therefore, became the world's leading industrial country in 1913, producing more than one-third of the world's industrial production (Walton and Rockoff 2014: 300–301). In this process, the proliferating corporations turned to the commercial paper market, state banks, and trust funds to fund their financing needs as their financing requirements were far beyond the capacity of banks due to restrictions on loan size.

At the end of the nineteenth century, the financial and production relations in the US economy were thus intermediated and dominated by the speculative financial markets, a process continuing with financial innovations out of which a more sophisticated and over risky financial regime emerged (Konings 2011: 26–53). Further, as banks were chartered for their investment-banking subsidiaries, regulatory initiatives in restricting banks' involvement in the security market, particularly in the aftermath of the crisis of 1873, did not yield any result. Furthermore, stock exchanges were then self-regulated cartels as there was no legislation or any regulatory authority for monitoring the trading of securities (Orhangazi 2008: 24–40).

The gold standard of 1870 and 1914, contrary to widespread belief, did not discipline but strengthened the organization of ever-increasing liquidity creation and financial innovation through the institutional axes of New York banks, the call loan market, and the stock market. This uncontrolled expansion and deepening, which was not harnessed by the Treasury and the New York Clearing House, triggered the panic of 1907, which saw bank runs, a scramble for liquidity, a freezing up of the market for call loans, a stock market meltdown, and the suspension of convertibility. This ensued in the creation of the Federal Reserve System in 1913 to restore financial order.

Until the twentieth century, on the other hand, securities were issued by governments and then by corporations only with the last quarter of the nineteenth century, traded between wealthy individuals and institutions, their bankers, and brokers. Ordinary people engaged in securities trade with their incomes rising only in the early twentieth century. Moreover, banks intermediated this trading during the 1920s with the New York Stock Exchange taking the initiative in providing American citizens with access to the prospects of ownership. However, this relationship weakened toward the end of the decade especially with the financialization of consumer credit. (Citizens were involved in the game not only as investors but also as borrowers with no access to knowledge about the rules, which was to cause the burning of ordinary people in the boom and bust of the 1920s.) The credit ordinary people could get consisted of, initially, only that secured by real estate. However, during the post-World War I period, other forms of financial intermediation became available, such as installment credit, applied not only to mortgages but also to a whole range of consumer durable goods.

The Federal Reserve (Fed) failed in streamlining the above summarized stock of financial governance. The Bank failed in restructuring the financial architecture that triggered the panic of 1907, in particular by limiting commercial banks' access to capital markets or challenging the underlying structures of the Money Trust on Wall Street. The Fed also could not quell or alleviate the bank failures by increasing the liquid reserves of the financial system and acting as a lender of last resort to the illiquid but solvent banks. Consequently, from the mid-1920s onward, speculative action in the financial markets peaked and caused the stock market crash in October 1929, the Great Depression. The value of banks' stock in investment collapsed, brokers defaulted massively on call loans, and many corporations and individuals defaulted on their bank loans (Konings 2011: 54–69).

2.4   Systemic Governance of US Economic Growth, 1948–1972

After the Great Depression, the New Deal from 1933 to 1939 aimed to increase the scope of the federal government's activities by way of harnessing the NICs of the laissez-faire period through regulating the financial and product markets, imposing tax codes, and conducting public programs. As a corollary, during the post-war period, the major target of the federal government's economic policy was to provide full employment via the Employment Act of 1946. Further, another important aspect of the Act was the establishment of the Council of Economic Advisers (CEA) to coordinate this policy. In this section, the performance consequences of economic, financial, and corporate governance during the FEP are discussed in comparison with the NLP.

We entitle the period from 1948 to 1972 as FEP because it was drawn on the deployment of factors of production at maximum rates to strike a workable trade-off between efficiency and equity. During this period, as illustrated in Table 2.1, the US economy generated higher growth and lower unemployment even with a much lower rate of inflation in the FEP than those in the NLP—a key indicator is that the output gap was 0.8 percent and minus 1.3 percent in the FEP and in the NLP, respectively (a negative and positive output gap indicates deficient and excess demand, resulting in lower and higher inflation, respectively).

Approximately two-thirds of the decline in federal tax revenues during the NLP is attributable to the decreasing rate of corporate tax revenues. Federal taxes on corporate income, the rate of which has been higher than the OECD average for over more than six decades, dropped from 4 percent of the GDP during the FEP to 2 percent in the NLP. The taxes on production and imports also declined from 2.3 percent of the GDP in the former to 1 percent in the latter. Apparently, the key reason underlying the sharp plummet in both kinds of taxes is, inter alia, nearly a quarter decline of private domestic investment as of real GDP during the NLP compared to the FEP. Furthermore, the average rate of annual borrowing by nonfinancial and financial sectors increased considerably during the NLP. As a result, the outstanding debt of these sectors rose to approximately 60 percent during the NLP from 37 percent and 7 percent, respectively.

The *tax state* of the FEP aimed mainly at developing the funds necessary to finance government expenditure as well as public programs for the low-income and unemployed. In socioeconomic terms, the FEP thus makes sense with its inclusive growth. Inclusive growth is defined as 'economic

Table 2.1 Macroeconomic indicators of American economy, 1948–2015

Series name	1948–1972	1973–1979	1980–2006	2007–2015
GDP per capita (billion $)	18,376	26,515	37,791	49,163
GDP growth	*4.0*	*3.4*	*3.1*	*1.3*
Government expenditures	0.9	0.3	0.4	0.0
Consumption expenditures	2.4	2.0	2.2	1.1
Private investment expenditures	0.8	0.9	0.7	0.0
Net exports	−0.1	0.2	−0.3	0.2
Budgetary balance[a]	−0.4	−2.2	−2.5	−5.3
Consumer Price Inflation	2.4	8.2	3.9	1.8
Unemployment	4.8	6.5	6.1	7.2
Money Stock (M2)	8.0	9.1	6.0	6.4
Interest[b]	4.6	8.9	9.0	4.0
Gross Savings[a]	22.7	22.4	19.6	16.9
Government	2.8	0.3	0.0	−3.7
Domestic business	11.2	12.2	12.3	13.8
Household	9.4	9.9	7.3	6.8
Debt outstanding by sector[a]				
Government	60.7	41.4	59.0	88.8
Households	37.4	46.2	64.9	87.2
Nonfinancial business	37.5	51.3	59.8	68.7
Domestic financial sector	7.4	17.7	58.8	100.5

Source: Bureau of Economic Analysis (2017), Economic Report of the President (1990, 2016)
[a]As percent of GDP
[b]Average of three- and ten-year bond interest rates

growth that creates opportunity for all segments of the population and distributes the dividends of increased prosperity, both in monetary and nonmonetary terms, fairly across society' (OECD 2014: 80). For example, hourly compensation increase in the nonfarm business sector, 2.8 percent, in the FEP was by and large tantamount to labor productivity increase of 2.6 percent. The same rates were 2.1 percent and 1.1 percent during the NLP, respectively (Bureau of Labor Statistics 2017a).

As Table 2.2 illustrates, the Gini coefficient for the country increased remarkably during the NLP compared to the FEP. The lowest, second, and third fifth echelons incurred the highest declines in their incomes. The highest fifth reaped income accruing from these echelons. Underlying

Table 2.2 Shares of aggregate income and Gini coefficient in the United States, 1967–2015

Year	Shares of aggregate income							Rate of change in marginal income tax for the top decile	Gini coefficient for households
	Lowest fifth	Second fifth	Third fifth	Fourth fifth	Highest fifth	Top 5 percent	Top 1 percent		
2007–2015	3.2	8.4	14.5	23.2	50.7	21.9	17.5	−16.2	0.47
1980–2006	3.7	9.3	15.5	23.8	47.7	19.8	12.9	−41.4	0.44
1973–1979	4.2	10.3	16.9	24.6	43.9	16.7	7.9	−14.7	0.40
1967–1972	4.1	10.8	17.4	24.5	43.3	16.7	8.9	–	0.39

Source: U.S. Census Bureau (2017); Piketty (2013: 499)

is, inter alia, the sharp declines in the top marginal tax rates for the top decile, illustrating the amount of tax received on each additional unit of income. The change in the same rate for Germany and France during the same period was only minus 5 percent and 0 percent, respectively (Piketty 2013; Saez and Piketty 2003). Effectively, these two data demonstrate that the FEP was strongly more inclusive than the NLP.

Among the key institutional changes after the Great Depression that made inclusive growth possible during the FEP was the enactment of a new system of industrial relations (IRs) with the National Labor Relations Act of 1935 mainly to guarantee workers with certain rights such as the opportunity to get organized into trade unions, establishment of a national minimum wage (first in 1933 and re-established in 1938), retirement benefits, compulsory federal health insurance, old-age insurance, unemployment benefits, increased federal allowances for housing, and so on (Hacker and Pierson 2010: 56). The New Deal reforms consolidated and expanded through the 1950s and 1960s. However, during the FEP, it was mainly national defense expenditures that made up half of total federal expenditures, whereas health, social security, income security, and medicare expenditures constituted only one-fifth of it. This budgetary imbalance between defense and social expenditures was reversed during the NLP.

In this regard, the FEP's inclusiveness crystallized mainly in the employment regime. Employment relationship during this period was a paternalistic form of welfare capitalism, providing stable employment, relatively high wages, low turnover, occupational training, and administered rules. A sign of this paternalism in the public sector was the remarkably higher rate of public employment, 22 percent in total between 1945 and 1972. This rate then declined to 9.5 percent between 1979 and 2015 (Bureau of Labor Statistics 2017b). As for the private sector, white-collar salaried employees had relative job security and promotion rights in return for organizational commitment and loyalty. In addition to white-collar workers, firms did not expose the blue-collar to hostile layoffs but provided them promotions based on seniority. In addition, four-fifths of the employment pattern during the FEP was permanent, and it changed only marginally during the NLP (OECD 2016a).

These opportunities were, nonetheless, tied to individual rather than collective contracts, and the union or employees did not have board-level representation. Underlying this was not only that the trade union density, 26 percent during the period 1960–1979, averaged much lower than that in the developed European countries, but that there did not emerge a dynamic of economic or industrial democracy in the US model from the scratch. Instead, in tandem with the type of workplace unionism, organized labor in the United States negotiated higher wages and social benefits through collective contracts at the company level. Further, the proportion of employees covered by wage bargaining agreements in total, collective bargaining coverage, was 30 percent in 1970, two to three times lower than that in the Scandinavian countries, Germany, France, and Italy. The coverage rate declined to 13 percent in 2010, at least five to eight times lower than in the latter countries (Thelen 2014: 37–47). Despite these loopholes, this relatively reasonable nature of employment relations resulted in the above-noted trade-off between labor productivity and real wages during the FEP.

The growth-driven and inclusive structure of the country's PE during the FEP rested upon a mass production regime under a managerial mode of corporate governance. From the late nineteenth century through the post-war period, mass production was the driving force of industrial efficiency through specialization, economies of scale, and a standardized system of production. In the large and homogenous markets, mass production, made by vertically integrated firms in high volumes, was price-driven, stable, and resistant to change. Interfirm cooperation was poor with underdeveloped trade associations with limited power to discipline their members. Work skills were narrowly defined and very specific, and the hierarchical employee-employer relationship was based on low trust and poor communication between labor and management. Moreover, the overarching priority of market regulation was to spur productive competition and weaken cartels (Hollingsworth 1999; Hirst and Zeitlin 1991).

Under such a regime of production, corporate governance in the United States was aligned with strong managers and weak owners. Top managers and employees were the long-term assets of corporations rather than as agents of shareholders or short-term responsibilities, respectively.

With the separation of corporate ownership and management, beginning with the 1930s, the latter became the primary actor in making and executing corporate affairs under the Fordist mode of production structure. Individual share ownership remained dominant during the post-war period, 94 percent and 67 percent in 1946 and 1975, respectively. The shareholder model and hostile takeovers were yet to hold sway by 1970— individual ownership was gradually substituted, 25 percent in 2007 with pension funds, mutual funds, insurance funds, and foreign investors. Corporate boards were mainly occupied by insiders, selected predominantly by owners rather than by shareholders from the company or former executives, whose decisions had only advisory value. In most privately held companies, executive remuneration consisted mainly of fixed salaries and bonuses commensurate with the company's productivity (Jackson 2010; Hilt 2014). This was not a stakeholder model of the German kind but a managerial one with quasi-stakeholder characteristics. Further, the profits of firms were not a source of capital market speculation but a source of reinvestment in the firm itself, generating one-quarter more private investment during the FEP than the NLP.

In financial terms, what complemented a growth-driven and inclusive private investment during the FEP were a regulated financial system and an accommodative monetary policy. The financial structure in the FEP rested mainly on regulations created during the New Deal period. The banking industry witnessed substantial reforms: first, the Federal Deposit Insurance Corporation (FDIC) insured public deposits in banks. Second, the Glass-Steagall Act of 1933 effectively decoupled investment and commercial banking activities, thereby preventing the undue diversion of publicly insured deposits into high-risk speculative operations by investment banks. In addition, the Act tightened branching restrictions, imposed interest rate ceilings on deposits, and empowered the Federal Reserve Board to vary reserve requirements (Vietor 2000: 979). In addition, the Securities and Exchange Commission (SEC) enforced the new market and securities laws: first, the commission protected ordinary investors by enforcing mandatory standardized disclosure of financial information, and second, preventing manipulation and insider trading. This model prevented systemic failures in the banking system from the 1930s through the 1960s (Sylla 2007: 139–141), except individual cases.

Under this regulatory system, the financial sector's share in the country's GDP was nearly two-thirds of that in the NLP. Specifically, the total share of the finance and insurance sectors was 80 percent less than that in the NLP. In addition, during the FEP, profitability of the financial sector was higher than the nonfinancial sector, but tolerable in terms of higher-risk exposure in the former. However, the same rate soared to 80 percent during the period 1991–2006, in particular to 127 percent between 2002 and 2006. The recovery rate of profits in financial sector from its downward trend in the 1980s was stronger than that in nonfinancial sector that has yet to recover to the high rates manifested in the 1960s (Bakir and Campbell 2013). The relative trade-off between the profitability in the two sectors, mainly during the 1960s, is a major reason for private domestic investment during the FEP to be more than one-quarter higher than that in the NLP, as noted above. Further, the same trade-off can be suggested to underlie additional two things.

First, market capitalization reached around only 40 percent, less than half of that in the NLP (the World Bank defines market capitalization [also known as market value], as the share price times the number of shares outstanding [including their several classes] for listed domestic companies, and the value of shares traded as the total number of shares traded, both domestic and foreign, multiplied by their respective matching prices). Second, personal income receipts on financial assets in the former were more than 40 percent lower compared to those in the latter. By inhibiting over-financialization, these two points factored in the sustainability of growth-driven and inclusive nature of the FEP.

In such a relatively less-financialized setting in the FEP, during the early 1950s, the Fed pursued an independent but active monetary policy focusing on bank credits and speeding them up during a contraction and slowing them down during an expansion, consistent with the real bills doctrine. The underlying rationale was that commercial bills could not be issued in excessive amounts as they were used to finance commercial transactions. Thus, they could not be inflationary but 'the other loans might encourage speculation and thus could be excessive'. Such a strategy aimed to foster sustainable growth without inflation mainly by moderating pressure on bank reserves (Meulendyke 1998: 24). Likewise, in line with a growth-driven structure, the real interest rates on both short-term and long-term treasury securities and the discount and lending interest rates, as well as federal funds rate in the NLP, ranged between nearly two-fifths and one-half of those in the NLP (U.S. President 2016: 428).

Inflationary pressure, however, accelerated in the late 1960s, which was argued to have arisen out of budget deficits due to the financing of the US involvement in the Vietnam War and social expenditures as well as the expansionary economic policy. The trend of rising inflation resulted in the outflow of official gold holdings, making the Bretton Woods system of pegged exchange rates less viable. In response, the Fed officially adopted monetary aggregates targeting its basic macroeconomic strategy in 1970, the primary guide for which was the federal funds rate. Despite tightened on several occasions, money stock however exceeded the target rates due to high inflation and declining rate of growth and employment in particular between 1975 and 1977 when unemployment soared to 8 percent on an average. Thus, during the 1970s, the various policy guidelines remained ineffective in containing inflation during due to, inter alia, the first and second oil price shocks and rapid growth in the Fed's portfolio.

2.5 Institutional Fragmentation in the US Model, 1973–2006

During the GSP, as noted earlier, the institutional underpinnings of the FEP became fragmented. This fragmentation then became embedded in the NLP. The NLP has been aligned with a neoclassical economic policy and finance-driven corporate governance contrasted sharply with the demand-side and growth-driven one in the FEP. A neoclassical economic policy is conducted through a tight fiscal and monetary policy drawn on inflation targeting, independent from the political authority and separated from regulatory activities such as banking supervision. The underlying rationale for the Republicans, proponents of this policy, was that neoclassical economic policy is a set of policy instruments that would boost output and employment, result in tax increases on incomes and savings, and create more prosperity for the entire society. The outcome, however, was different, not only because this period ended up with the Great Recession of 2007–2009 but also that the performance indicators are evidently poorer than those in the NLP.

The basic indicator for the tight fiscal policy pursued in the NLP is a more than twofold decline in government expenditures than those in the FEP. Despite the consequent more than twofold decline in the contribution of government expenditures to economic growth, the budgetary deficit increased more than fivefold, government savings dropped to zero, and government borrowing as an annual average soared more than twofold in the NLP than that in the FEP. The government debt was 60 percent of the GDP in the NLP, on a par with that in the FEP.

During the NLP, the key monetary policy strategy was *post hoc interventionism*. This policy is based on the notion that bubbles are difficult to spot correctly and that a bubble, if any, could be effectively controlled only after it bursts. Further, preventative pricking of bubbles could result in an unnecessary economic contraction. As a result, in contrast to the growth-driven monetary policy in the FEP, post hoc interventionism focused mainly on sustaining price stability. With this mindset, the Fed is argued to have responded more systematically than it had earlier to deviations of inflation and output from their desired levels.

> Prior to the Great Moderation, monetary policy often followed what was called a "go-stop" policy. In general, monetary policy was eased to fight recessions during the "go-phase" and was tightened to combat rising inflation during the "stop-phase." However, prior to the Great Moderation, the Fed would often maintain easy policy for too long leading to higher inflation. It would then tighten policy to fight rising inflation, but not for long enough. As a result, inflation generally rose in an erratic pattern during the 1960s and 1970s. By reducing the episodes of "go—stop" policies, a more systematic monetary policy reduces volatility. Changes in the Federal Reserve's approach to communicating about its monetary policy probably also contributed to the Great Moderation. Better communication and more transparency meant monetary policy could be more effective, for example, by better anchoring inflation expectations, which allows policy to have greater flexibility in responding to short-run developments. Asset prices would reflect the systematic part of policy, which also has a stabilizing influence. (Hakkio 2013)

Validity of the Fed's policy argument, as noted by Hakkio (2013), can be observed in the trend of the *go-stop* policy, specifically between the mid-1960s and the late 1970s, and the trend of *systematic* policy between the early 1980s and the Great Recession. In the latter period, there were only one year of downward and upward deviations from the trend, particularly in 1987, 1998, and 2001 against the larger and longer volatilities in the former period between 1964 and 1978. As Table 2.1 illustrates, a nonaccommodative monetary policy did not yield a lower level of inflation in the NLP than in the FEP despite the lack of a supply shock, but contributed to approximately a one-quarter lower rate of growth and employment than in the FEP (there is an outright *inflation and employment illusion* arising out of the comparison of inflation and unemployment rates during the NLP and the Stagflation of the 1970s rather than those during the former and the FEP). Nor did the asset prices play a stabilizing role as a systematic part of the monetary policy, as can be seen in the sharp rise and decline of home prices between 2005 and 2008, the underlying cause of the Great Recession. In contrast, home prices and stock prices turned out to be quite stable in the FEP, except during the period 1948–1954 (Figs. 2.1 and 2.3).

Furthermore, the Fed's failure was not limited to contributing toward a negative output gap of minus 1.3 percent in the NLP as a *sacrifice* for the lower level of inflation than that during the Stagflation of the 1970s. The Bank also directly contributed to the genesis of the ongoing Great Recession by shunning a proactive regulatory discretion primarily due to regulatory capture, unquestioned free-market ideology, the use of mathematical models with little relevance for actual financial developments, and a narrow focus on inflation targeting. After a comprehensive examination of the Fed's policy documents, Golub et al. (2015: 659) conclude that 'Strikingly, research and policy deliberation very infrequently touched on the financial activities that are now known to have led to the collapse'. As a corollary, the Financial Crisis Inquiry Commission (FCIC) (2011:3) notes that:

> Ben Bernanke, the chairman of the Federal Reserve Board since 2006, told the Commission a "perfect storm" had occurred that regulators could not have anticipated; but when asked about whether the Fed's lack of aggressiveness in regulating the mortgage market during the housing boom was a

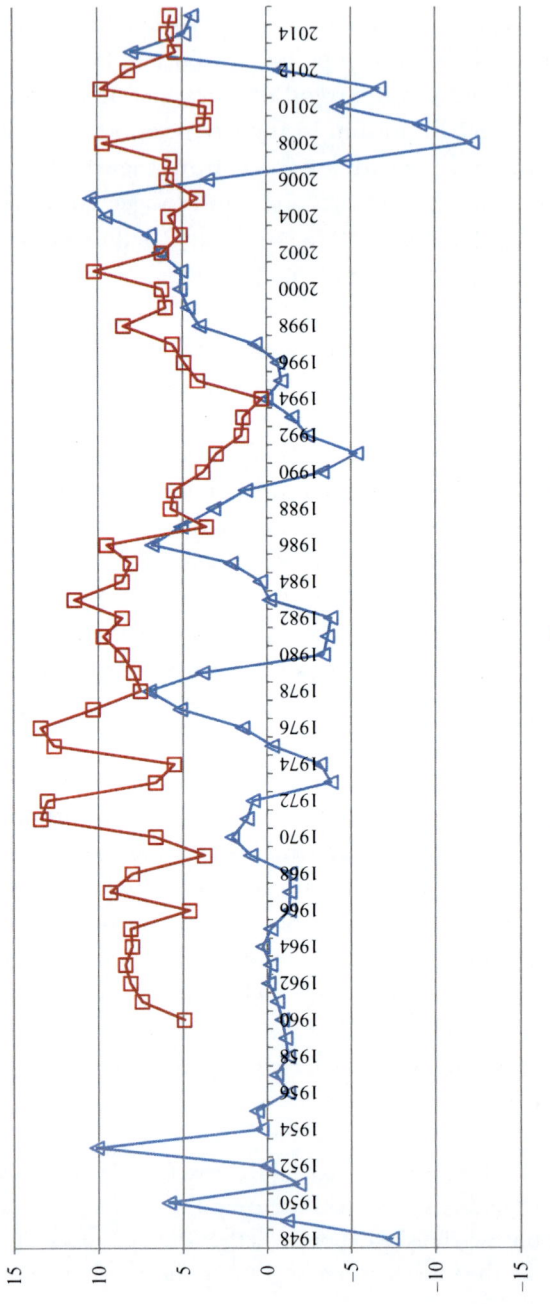

Fig. 2.1 Home prices and money growth in the United States, annual change %, 1948–2015. Source: Fed (2017a); Schiler (2009)

failure, Bernanke responded, "It was, indeed. I think it was the most severe failure of the Fed in this particular episode." Alan Greenspan, the Fed chairman during the two decades leading up to the crash, told the Commission that it was beyond the ability of regulators to ever foresee such a sharp decline. "History tells us [regulators] cannot identify the timing of a crisis, or anticipate exactly where it will be located or how large the losses and spillovers will be".

Greenspan earlier thought that 'The market-stabilizing private regulatory forces should gradually displace many cumbersome, increasingly ineffective government structures' (FCIC 2011: 38). But, in his Congressional hearing of October 2008, he noted that 'Those of us who have looked to the self-interest of lending institutions to protect shareholders' equity, myself included, are in a state of shocked disbelief.' He also responded, 'Yes, I've found a flaw. I don't know how significant or permanent it is. But I've been very distressed by that fact,' to the question of whether he thought that his ideology had misled him (NYT 2008).

Ex post, there are a couple of widely accepted causes of today's recession in the country: the lack of a proactive regulatory action; failure of risk management in the financial system and in corporate governance; the existence of a combination of excessive borrowing, risky investments, as well as lack of transparency; a systemic breakdown in accountability and ethics; and so on. The FCIC also agreed to these points, which are explained as follows.

First, there are a number of legislations underlying financial deregulations beginning with the early 1970s: (1) in 1970, investment banks were allowed to sell their shares on the exchanges, (2) interest rate ceilings that banks and other lenders could charge were made dependent by the Supreme Court rule in 1978 only on the usury laws in their home state, (3) commercial banks were allowed to pay interest on checkable deposits in 1980, (4) the saving and loan industry was deregulated and banks were allowed to provide adjustable-rate mortgages in 1983, and (5) restrictions on the establishment of nationwide commercial banks were repealed in 1994.

Most importantly, large parts of the Glass-Steagall Act of 1933 were repealed after the Financial Services Modernization Act of 1999 (FSM) was enacted, allowing the merger of investment banks, commercial banks, and insurance companies under a new entity. In addition, the Commodities Futures Modernization Act of 2000 did not bring any regulatory constraint on transactions involving over-the-counter derivatives. The SEC started implementing its net capital exemption rule in 2004, enabling Wall Street's largest brokerage houses and investment banks to self-regulate their operations in terms of assessing the value of their capital at risk.

A deregulated asset-backed securities market that boomed, as illustrated in Fig. 2.2, under this institutional setting urged excessive leverage and risk-taking by financial firms and the banking sector, and evergrowing funds for the mortgage markets (Campbell 2011: 220–223). The share of home mortgages in the total liability of households and nonprofit organizations nearly doubled, 44 percent of the GDP on average, in the NLP than in the FEP. This was a debt-financed investment, increasing household indebtedness from 37 percent as of GDP on an average in the FEP to 70 percent in the NLP. Thus, personal savings, as of disposable income, decreased from 11 percent in the FEP to 7 percent in the NLP. To tempt households to do that, the incentive for mortgage

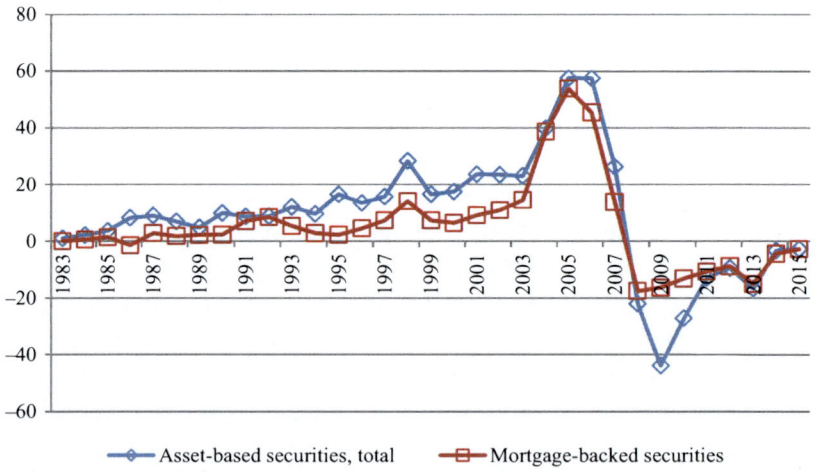

Fig. 2.2 Total asset-backed and mortgage-backed securities as % of GDP, 1983–2015. Source: Fed (2017a)

borrowing was increased from the 1970s onward. First, the administration of President Lyndon Johnson organized Fannie Mae (Federal National Mortgage Association), Freddie Mac (Federal Home Loan Mortgage Corporation), and Ginnie Mae (Government National Mortgage Association) to lend money and hold mortgages as well as to insure those mortgages against the risk of default. In 1970, to eliminate the risk for the government to hold those mortgages for too long, a new form of mortgage-backed securities (MBS) was invented with the financial services industry, and then the 1986 Tax Reform Act permitted the issuance of MBS. In addition, the same Act also allowed unlimited interest deduction for mortgages on both first and second homes.

What further expanded this market and increased its riskiness was that in the early 2000s Fannie and Freddie began purchasing huge swaths of subprime mortgages. Banks and mortgage companies issued these mortgages, thereby providing a market for subprime loans. This institutional expansion of the public-led housing finance occurred due to the Bush administration's strategy in enabling the financially strapped middle and working classes to own their homes. Furthermore, the Bush administration also capped the mortgage lending that Fannie and Freddie could make. Thus, in view of public support and the regulatory limits to Fannie and Freddie's lending, mortgage lenders rushed to make these risky loans as 'they could turn around and sell them to Fannie and Freddie'. Finally, mortgage companies pressured loan officers to lend risky borrowers on weak credibility or collaterals. Inducing them to do so was that the riskiest mortgages could also be turned into asset-backed securities and then sold to investors. Thus, they were able to capitalize on the commission without undertaking any organizational risk (Campbell, 217–220).

The crisis started in the subprime market where the high-yield and riskier mortgages were given to poorer and less creditworthy households to provide them access to finance and refinance their homes by collateralizing these mortgages. This strategy worked as long as the home prices kept increasing till 2006, but once prices started to plummet, the cycle fell into default (Fig. 2.2). Combined with the extremely high indebtedness and low savings ratio of the households, this sharp decline ended up with more than a 50 percent decrease in private consumption expenditures during the period from 2007 to 2015 compared to that in the NLP (average borrowing by households per annum as a percentage of GDP declined to 1.1 percent in the period 2007–2015 from 5.4 percent in the NLP). Further, the contribution of private consumption expenditure to economic growth declined to zero in the period 2007–2015 (see Table 2.1).

The subprime crisis spread across the entire financial system because the securitized subprime credits were of low quality and overly complex and had been assembled, packaged, and sliced into tranches with various levels of risk. Banks invested in these assets and used the income stream to service their debt. In addition, the incentive pay structures in financial firms that were drawn on the commissions, transactions, and bonuses were paid out of the profits. Thus, brokers and bankers focused not on good lending but on loan pushing irrespective of the loan repayments. Consequent excessive leverage or extreme debt-to-equity ratio among investment banks became the key source of financial fragility in rolling over the debts with the declining prices of asset-backed securities.

The investment bank leverage (debt-to-equity) ratios soared to over 30 and 1 by 2008 from around 15 and 1 in 2004. Of the big five Wall Street investment banks, Goldman Sachs had liabilities that were close to 30 times of its capital, while that of others ranged between 36 percent and 39 percent. The US commercial banks' leverage ratios were relatively lower due to 'resorting to off balance sheet vehicles kept outside the consolidation perimeter thanks to indulgent accounting rules' (Palley 2012: 60–61; Carmassi et al. 2009: 982). The result was the sector's net acquisition of short-term loans from the Federal Reserve System, 2.3 trillion and 2.9 trillion dollars in the third and fourth quarters of 2008, respectively. The domestic financial sector's total debt increased from 58 percent of the country's GDP during the NLP to 100 percent in the GRP.

In addition to the deregulated financial setting, the Fed also contributed to the genesis of the crisis by its failure in managing money supply. Monetary policy was accommodative in the latter part of the 1990s but turned aggressively expansionary in the 2000s (see Fig. 2.1), and nominal interest rates were below the levels indicated by the Taylor Rule, as was the case in mortgage interest rates during the late 1980s and the early 2000s. This triggered speculative bubbles by accelerating credit boom and asset prices (a speculative bubble is 'a widespread or generalized increase in asset prices to unsustainable levels' [Carmassi et al. 2009: 982]). The Fed opposed specifying asset prices with its post hoc interventionist perspective. As can be seen in Fig. 2.1, housing prices peaked to a permanently high plateau, particularly between 1998 and 2006 after which they started declining and plummeted in 2007 and 2008. Further, the home market accumulated a bubble in the former period because there was a sharp increase in MBS with strong positive expectations over house prices during the so-called high plateau period.

Financial deregulation wreaked havoc on the nonfinancial corporate business, not through excessive leverage but over-financialization. After a remarkably high leverage ratio in the 1980s, the sector reduced its incurrence of liabilities especially with the 2001 recession, turning into a net lender between 2001 and 2004. There was only a one-year steep increase in the (nonfinancial) corporate businesses' leverage in 2007, but the increasing trend of leverage sharply reversed in 2008 when the crisis spilled into the real economy.

There are two pillars of the financialization of corporate governance in the country. The first is market capitalization of corporate finance reaching 140 percent of GDP with a rapid increase from 40 percent in 1980. This increase unfolded in parallel with the asset price bubbles, as stock market prices skyrocketed from the early 1980s until 2000 when the market surged nearly eight-fold, as shown in Fig. 2.3. There were subsequent boom periods between 2003–2007 and 2009–2015. A similar boom was the case for the S&P Composite earnings in the 1990s and between the years 2003–2007 (Fig. 2.4). A significant consequence of market capitalization in a fluid market structure is that the handover duration of shares declined from seven years in the 1940s to two years in 1987 and to seven months in 2007 (Stiglitz 2016: 46).

The second pillar of financialization is the increasing size, speculative structure, and yields of corporate bond markets. In response to rising inflation during the 1970s, the commercial paper market and the money market mutual funds grew in size by the late 1970s (money market mutual funds invest in short-term liquid assets such as commercial papers). In terms of G&D, the significance of this growth lies in financing companies in the nonfinancial sector. These companies increased the size of short-term bonds with a maturity of less than one year to obtain

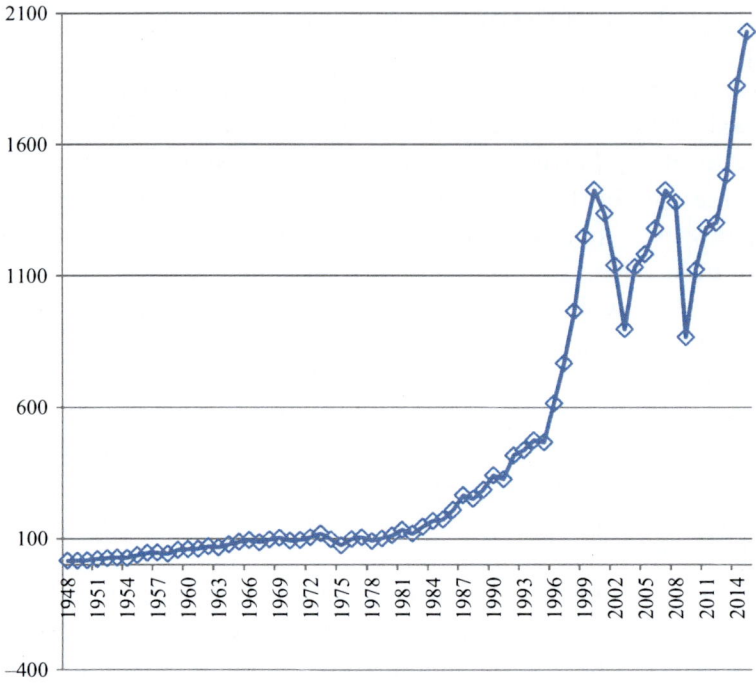

Fig. 2.3 Stock prices in the United States, annual change %, 1948–2015. Source: Schiler (2009)

financing in the commercial paper market. Moreover, money market mutual funds bought these bonds as they, in particular those rated BAA, were more attractive to bank depositors due to paying a higher interest rate than bank deposits, home mortgages, as well as treasury securities of both long- and short-term maturities. Thus, it became possible for less creditworthy corporations to access financing with innovations in the junk bond market, stimulating a riskier, high-yield investment appetite (Palley 2012: 57–59). The yields of corporate bonds rated AAA increased from 4 percent in the FEP to 9 percent in the NLP (the same rates for those rated BAA were 5 percent and 10 percent, respectively).

For two reasons, financialization acts as a NIC for economic growth in the United States. First, it generates higher profits in shorter maturities in the financial sector than the nonfinancial (Arrighi 1994; Krippner 2005).

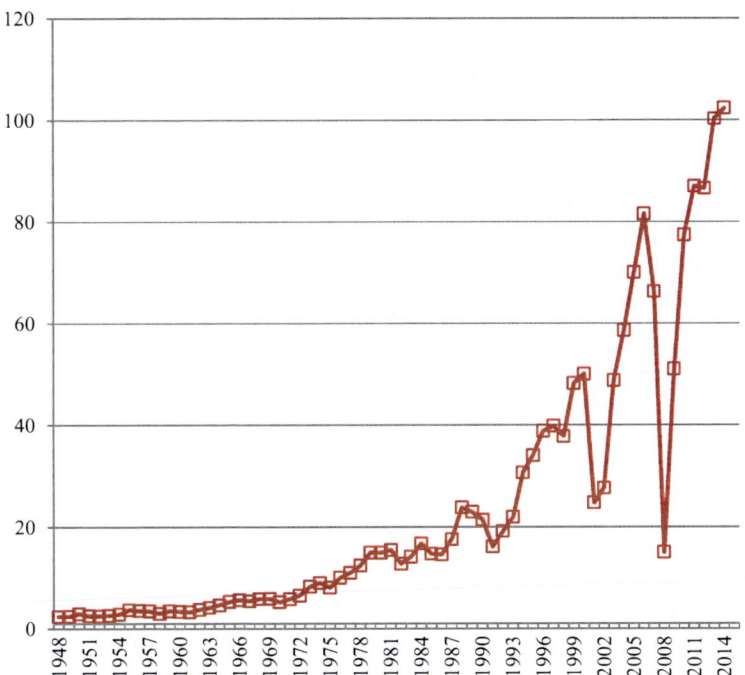

Fig. 2.4 Stock earnings in the United States, annual change %, 1948–2015. Source: Schiler (2009)

Second, it drives corporate governance into a short-term orientation by imposing shareholder value rather than growth and employment as the independent variable of doing business. These two aspects have factored in (1) the plummeting share of the manufacturing sector versus the increasing share of the financial sector in the country's GDP and (2) the increasing volatility ending up with the GRP and the GSNP (Tables 2.1 and 2.3).

There are two instruments of a shareholder model of corporate governance that subjected corporate businesses to short-term and risky financial gains, thereby excluding a private investment structure facilitated by growth and innovation. The first is an incentive structure that tied executive compensation to share prices instead of profits. This incited CEOs, whose job tenure has become shorter on average to generate ever-higher

Table 2.3 Financial indicators of American economy as % of GDP, 1950–2015

Series name	1950–1972	1973–1979	1980–2006	2007–2015
Market capitalization of listed domestic companies	–	40.6	87.1	120.9
Personal income receipts on assets	8.3	11.6	14.9	13.0
Value added of financial sector to the GDP	13.2	14.7	18.2	19.8
Finance and insurance	3.5	4.4	6.3	6.8
Real estate, rental, and leasing	9.7	10.3	11.9	13.0
Financial profits as % of total corporate profits	16.6	17.4	25.5	24.8

Source: Federal Reserve (2017a); Bureau of Economic Analysis (2017); World Bank (2017)

share prices, to take excessive risks and design accounting tricks, particularly in the finance sector, to increase executive pay and payouts to stockholders. In order to motivate CEOs to enforce a shareholder model, astronomic increases were made in executive compensation at the expense of workers, real investment, and shareholders. Executives of nonfinancial companies now constitute 30 percent in the top 1 percent of the income ladder. The average real CEO pay was largely constant at around US$ one million from the 1930s through the mid-1970s. The same rate for the 500 highest-paid CEOs was US$ 30.3 million in 2012. Only 6.3 percent of this pay consisted of salaries and bonuses and the rest of gains from stocks and stock options. Compared to employee pay, CEO pay was 20 times higher in 1965. This rate skyrocketed to 295 times by 2013. What made this possible at the corporate level are the changes made in federal income tax, pension, corporate governance, and securities laws that reinforced the power of institutional investors and tied executive pay to short-term returns (Stiglitz 2016; OECD 2009).

Second, leveraged buyouts enable investors aiming to make large acquisitions (almost half of all major US companies experienced hostile takeover bids during the 1980s). Toward this, *corporate raiders* widely used junk bonds to acquire companies and pay back the debt by selling its divisions. Interestingly, corporations with low share prices and large cash balances in stable-tech sectors incurred hostile takeovers in the

1980s, as they could sell their products at competitive prices while reducing reinvestment. In these sectors, managers embarked on increasing the level of dividend payouts and engaging in large-scale stock repurchases to push up share prices (Lazonick 2005: 589; Holstrom and Kaplan 2001). Broadly, the purpose of an acquisition is either to restructure the firms and sell it quickly or to reduce market competition. The latter became possible with the antitrust regulations across many sectors that are elaborated below beginning with the early 1970s.

The shareholder model of US kind, as a result, sparked off large corporate bankruptcies such as Enron and Worldcom, essentially due to their fraudulent financial reporting practices, coercing the Bush administration to enact the Sarbanes-Oxley Act of 2002. The Act aimed to ensure external auditors' independence and strengthen the board of directors' oversight of the company management by creating a new regulator, the Public Company Accounting Oversight Board (PCAOB). The PCAOB enforces professional standards of audits for companies by stipulating that the audit committee should report to the board of directors rather than the company's management (Sorenson and Miller 2017).

However, it now emerges that corporate governance structures and accounting standards had significant loopholes in safeguarding against excessive risk-taking in financial services and nonfinancial companies and that the boards did not fulfill their responsibility in overseeing risk management and the compatibility of remuneration and incentive systems with risk appetite (Kirkpatrick 2009). In view of these loopholes, the Dodd-Frank Act of 2010 empowered the SEC to ensure that a company includes shareholder nominees along with the company's candidates when it sends proxy materials to all of its shareholders before the annual meeting. In addition, shareholders are provided with a nonbinding vote on the compensation packages of the company's directors and top executives (Kim and Muldoon 2015: 97).

Complementing this short-termism in financial and corporate governance is the post-Fordist system of production regime. The fact that less developed countries with a higher labor costs were able to replicate standardized products and then sell them to the United States at lower prices led to the country's manufacturers losing their market share, though the demand for certain standardized goods remained stable. This trend created a transformative impact on the Fordist production systems toward the post-Fordist ones. Post-Fordism is a pattern of production, particularly in the technologically complex sectors under highly competitive and volatile markets, and is aligned with flexible and diversified quality specialization.

With the rise of post-Fordism, first, the market structure has become quality-driven, smaller, and more heterogeneous. Second, with vertical disintegration, firms form various obligatory networks, changed according to industries, with producers, processors, distributors, research institutes, business associations, local governments, and various types of credit institutions. Third, the production process has been diffused through high-trust contracts between subcontracting, cooperative contracting, joint ventures, and strategic alliances. Fourth, in accordance with quality-driven competition, the labor force is expected to be well-trained, highly flexible, and broadly skilled (Hollingsworth 1999; Hirst and Zeitlin 1991).

2.6   Industrial Policy: The Visible Hand of the US Model

Abraham Lincoln (1861–1865) adopted a growth-enhancing strategy using high tariffs as part of the strategic industrial policy, federal land grants, market-securing government procurement, and subsidized infrastructural development. Average tariff rates on manufactured products in the United States were around 40 percent between 1820 and 1931, three to four times higher than that in France, Germany, and Sweden (Bairoch 1993: 40). Lincoln's civil engineering project—the transcontinental railway of the 1860s—was one of the most ambitious in world history of that time. In addition, the federal and state governments supported R&D, which first began in the agriculture sector during the 1860s. From the turn of the nineteenth century, the government intervened to encourage the growth of cutting-edge mass market industries through procurement, standard setting, and supply of appropriate capabilities.

In the early twentieth century, the federal government's involvement continued with the airmail industry via fees to subsidize the infant civil aviation industry, with its procurement to help establish the early aircraft industry and advanced chemical sector, with the expansion of its commitment to agricultural research engineering training particularly after the World War I, and so on. Industrial policy thus played a key role in the fact that, from the early nineteenth century to the 1930s, the United States evolved into a leading industrial, trade, and financial power (Nester 1998: 122–162).

Industrial policy in the country then gained a more ordered structure with the New Deal by administering prices, increasing dialogue between stakeholders, harnessing the financial sector, and providing public infrastructure. In the run-up to the World War II, the US government's selective industrial policy intensified mainly in the form of basic research support of military laboratories in launching a series of fundamental innovations such as the atom bomb, hydrogen bomb, missile technology, civilian nuclear power, computers, the transistor, and satellites (Kozul-Wright 1995; Wade 2014).

In the first three-quarters of the twentieth century, the US government provided considerable support to a number of industries in the form of subsidies including the federal land grants made to railroads, tax exemption such as the depletion allowance on minerals, direct loans to farmers in 1916, the contracts for the construction of industrial facilities in World War II, and the promotion of research by governmental funds such as those allocated to the defense industry.

From the 1980s onward, similar programs and policies functioned mainly to forge networks and overcome network failures as well as to stimulate and sustain the formation and development of an innovation-driven economic capacity.

The post-1980 policies consist mainly of (1) fiscal incentives in the form of tax credits and incentives for various types of activities such as research and development, (2) investment attraction programs including efforts to generate regional or local industrial or technological clusters, (3) training policies including the Manufacturing Extension Program to provide consultation to small manufacturers, (4) infrastructure support, (5) trade measures by participating in multiple international or regional trade agreements, (6) public procurement in particular by the defense industry to nurture an array of industries, and (7) using financial mechanisms in the form of loans and risk sharing to invest in technologies and/ or early stage firms. In addition, after the housing bubble, industrial restructuring schemes were also used in major automakers and financial institutions as short-term emergency measures (Keller and Block 2011: 244–246; Wade 2012).

Above all, it has always been R&D support that underlies the US industrial policy. After World War II, the federal government dramatically expanded its industrial and academic research support. Total federal R&D expenditures increased to US$ 1313 million in 1945 from US$ 83 million in 1940. By 1969, R&D expenditures in the United States was US$ 25.6 billion, surpassing the combined R&D expenditures of then other largest industrial economies, US$ 11.3 billion (West Germany, France, the United Kingdom, and Japan), and it was not until the late 1970s that the latter exceeded the former. During the period 1953–1975, the share of federal and industry R&D expenditures was 58 percent and 39 percent, respectively. By 1990, the same rates were 47 percent and 48 percent, respectively. In addition to R&D, the federal government also contributed toward industrial innovation and progress via the post-war antitrust policy that enabled startup firms to enter into markets such as microelectronics and computers and military procurement that provided technological infrastructure and an important springboard for startup firms. Broadly, the country's R&D strategy over the last seven decades can be grouped under the following four policy areas (Keller and Block 2011).

First, the Defense Advanced Research Projects Agency (DARPA) was founded in 1958 to foresee and generate beyond the horizon technologies. The Agency supported R&D projects with modest funds, but in a targeted and selective manner. Second are the federal laboratories. The government continued funding the laboratories, founded earlier to develop nuclear weapons, with strong incentives to identify commercially promising technologies in the aftermath of the Cold War. Third are public-private partnerships. Underlying these partnerships is the contribution of universities and public research facilities to the advancements in technological and innovative dynamism; particularly, the Bayh-Dole Act of 1980 is an influential legislation that gives universities the right to patent their research developed using federal funding. Fourth are demand-side measures. The federal government has supported technology development through procurement, using a series of incentives to stimulate private sector demand.

Industrial Regulation and Deregulation

Industrial regulation to ensure the competitiveness of markets has a long history in the country dating back to the Interstate Commerce Commission, created in 1887 as the first national industrial regulatory body, and the Sherman Antitrust Act of 1890 that proscribed certain mergers and anticompetitive business practices. The Sherman Act, together with the Federal Trade Commission Act and the Clayton Act, both passed in 1914, forms the core of the federal antitrust law. They describe unlawful business practices in fairly general terms, leaving it to the courts to decide which specific acts are illegal on a case-by-case basis (Law and Kim 2011).

In the FEP, the United States built a federal regulatory state with a number of institutions to monitor anticompetitive practices and weigh challenges to monopoly behavior in all major sectors such as agriculture, manufacturing, finance, utilities, transportation, and natural resources. Underlying this wave of regulation was that an average 6 percent growth between 1921 and 1929 had created excess capacity, encouraging a more oligopolistic market competition. In sectors such as communications, transport, energy, and retail distribution, the New Deal regulatory constraints established a public policy regime of microeconomic stabilization with the aim of equity, fairness, or development instead of allocative efficiency and consumer sovereignty.

Then newly formed federal agencies were equipped with extraordinary powers to eliminate monopoly and intervene directly. In addition to anti-monopoly cases, antitrust agencies dealt with an ever-increasing number of price fixing and other cases of horizontal collusion, predatory pricing, and similar unfair practices. The rate of prosecution by the Justice Department, in this process, rose to 38 cases from 9 cases annually, one-third of which involved structural cases such as monopoly and anticompetitive mergers. Over the last three decades until the mid-1960s, albeit arising organizational inefficiencies in obtaining structural divestments and seeking criminal sentences, this regulatory setting became influential in striking a balance between destructive competition and monopoly abuse, thereby contributing to high growth and low inflation during this period.

However, with declining growth and accelerating inflation beginning with the late 1960s, firms faced a number of predicaments under the regulatory setting such as over-capitalization, debt leverage, a bias toward excess capacity, high costs, and cross-subsidized pricing schemes. Other factors that precipitated a deregulatory wave were emerging post-Fordism that required flexible and just-in-time production; technological innovations, particularly in the communication sector, that made substitutes available and lowered entry costs; and organizational inefficiencies of the regulatory bureaucracy that caused anti-regulatory circles to use courts, the regulatory arena, and legislative reforms to address structural changes of deregulation (Hirst and Zeitlin 1991).

Accordingly, in the 1970s, economic ideas in the field of competition were dominated by free-market scholars who viewed the antitrust regulation as antiquated and counterproductive in its effect on competition. The debate on deregulation was dominated by the members of the Chicago School who did not reject industrial concentration per se but confined the purpose of antitrust action to encourage competition. With the guidelines published by the US Department of Justice in 1968 for horizontal mergers and the establishment of a system by the Federal Trade Commission (FTC) for pre-merger notification reporting, and the formalization of this notification system under the Hart-Scott-Rodino Antitrust Improvements Act of 1976, the then government aimed to deregulate industrial competition in order to restore business confidence, in line with this view. Thus, many key industries, including financial services, airlines, railroads, telecommunications, petroleum and natural gas, electric power, and trucking, were deregulated from the 1970s through the 1990s, particularly during President Carter's era between 1977 and 1981 (Vietor 2000).

In such a deregulated environment, competition in the US industry has, however, been on the decline for these three reasons: growing industry concentration, increasing rents accruing to a few firms, and lower levels of firm entry and labor market mobility (CEA 2016). First, a key indicator available for market concentration is the percentage change in the share of revenue earned by the 50 largest firms. Between 1997 and 2012, that change ranged from 11.4 percent in transportation and warehousing to 9.9 percent in finance and insurance and 4.6 percent in utilities. In particular, the top ten banks' loan and deposit market shares increased from 30 percent and 20 percent in 1980, respectively, to 50 percent in 2010. As a result, the sector's annual profits turned out to be more than US$ 115 billion attributable to imposing higher-than-expected prices on their customers. Further, a greater part of these profits were transferred to top officials and other bankers, a major source of income inequality at the top (Stiglitz 2013: 58).

Second, between 1965 and 2014, the return on invested capital for firms at the 90th percentile among the publicly traded US nonfinancial firms increased more than fivefold than the median, which was closer just twofold at the beginning of the 1990s. Third, between 1980 and 2014, the ratio of firm entry to firm exit and the rate of net job creation declined from 28 percent and 6 percent in the late 1970s to 15 percent and 1.6 percent during the period 1980–2014, respectively. In particular, firm entry-exit rate during the years between 2007 and 2014 was around 10 percent, and the job creation rate plummeted to 0.5 percent (U.S. Census Bureau 2017).

The potential causes of declining market competition are, inter alia, firm behavior and occupational licensing. The US law offers government awards for temporary monopolies for their inventions under the patent system. Many firms have used this opportunity to earn profits by asserting royalty rights on patents. In addition, firms might attempt to increase their profits utilizing anticompetitive means such as colliding with rivals, purchasing competitors, erecting barriers to entry, and so on. Microsoft's trick over Netscape is a clear example of *colliding with rivals*. With its monopoly in PC operating systems, Microsoft embarked on eliminating the competitive threat posed by Netscape, which brought the browser to the market using government funds. Microsoft's Internet Explorer failed to overwhelm Netscape's Navigator. Microsoft used its monopoly power deploying a strategy known as FUD (fear, uncertainty, and doubt). The company did so, inter alia, by 'creating anxiety about compatibility among users by programming error messages that would randomly appear if Netscape was installed on a Windows computer … and it offered Internet Explorer at a zero price-free, bundled in as part of its operating system. It is hard to compete with a zero price. Netscape was doomed' (Stiglitz 2013: 57). Occupational licensing increased more than fivefold from the 1950s to the 2000s. Albeit a potential source of efficiency, it might also restrain workers' mobility across jobs and firms, thereby becoming a drag on the increase in labor market productivity.

Industrial Performance

The shareholder model approach to corporate governance has reduced the marginal propensity to invest in manufacturing with a productive and innovative potential. The value added of a manufacturing sector to the country's GDP reduced from 27 percent in the period 1947–1979 first to 17 percent in the NLP and to 12 percent during the Great Recession. Instead of producing within the country, many American firms locate their large integrated production units abroad with a focus on product design and marketing contracting with firms that are part of the regional production network in Asia, thereby undertaking only a small part of their own production (a key factor causing the US firms to locate their production plants overseas is corporate taxes in the United States, which has remained at 35 percent, whereas the OECD average declined from 30 percent to 22 percent in the period 2000–2016). For example, in the computer and electronics industry, the country's trade deficit with China increased to 56 percent in 2011 from 14 percent of gross industry output in 1998 (Baily and Bosworth 2014: 16). A leading example, Apple contracted with firms located in Taiwan and Korea to assemble its products in China to extract much of the profit by controlling the key elements in the value chain (Pierce and Schott 2014; Edwards and Lawrence 2013).

High productivity performance in the US economy stems largely from the tremendous increase of productivity in two sectors—computers and electronics. Excluding these two sectors, approximately 90 percent of the manufacturing sector's productivity rate has been fairly slow. In the period 1987–2011, the rates of GDP growth and the real value added in the manufacturing were 2.6 percent and 2.5 percent, respectively. When the computer and electronics sectors are excluded, the annual growth rate of the US manufacturing output during the same period declines to 0.6 percent, indicating the country's fragile competitive performance in industrial terms. The growth rate of these two sectors was 20 percent on an average, about 30 times higher than that in the rest of the manufacturing sector (however, during this period, the country's status in these two sectors changed from being the global leader to a large net importer of computers and peripheral documents). Similarly, productivity growth in the manufacturing sector, excluding computers, declined to 0.3 percent in the period 1987–2011. As noted earlier, labor productivity also declined from 2.6 percent in the FEP to 1.1 percent in the NLP, despite the sharp declines in unit labor costs during the latter.

In addition to the declining share of the manufacturing sector in the country's GDP, research and development intensity in high-tech manufacturing plummeted from 37 percent from 1987 to 28 percent in 2000, and steadily recovered to 36 percent in 2007 (however, this resurgence should be considered with the decreasing share of manufacturing value added). The country's expenditure in R&D, 2.6 percent during the period 1988–2013, lagged South Korea and Japan, 2.8 percent and 3.2 percent, respectively. The key issue is that, in parallel with the decline in manufacturing capacity, the country faces a decline in its high-tech productive potential and is losing market share due to growing competition from Asia. In particular, the US trade deficit with Asian countries rose from US$ 316 billion by 2000 to US$ 460 billion in 2012. This massive trade imbalance equals in value nearly half of the then manufacturing value added (Baily and Bosworth 2014).

The declining efficiency of US higher education has also wreaked havoc on industrial performance. Conventionally, education has not been subjected to central control by an organization such as a higher education council and, therefore, stimulated dynamic competition for students, faculty, resources, and prestige. The country's higher education institutions were always dependent on local sources for political and financial support that urged them to develop collaborative relationships with regional industrial and agricultural institutions to prepare a curriculum and research agenda in tandem with this relationship, and finally to train students for professional careers in the private sector. The tertiary level enrollment rate of 80 percent in the United States during the period 1990–2013 is far above the OECD average of 53 percent and, in fact, the second highest after Canada. However, first, the United States trails many other countries in developing effective vocational education and job-training programs, and the educational attainment of young workers is lagging than that of countries like Canada, Japan, and South Korea. Both the US and foreign companies investing in the United States report that the skill sets of the US workforce are comparatively weak. Second, since the early 1980s, college fees soared from a quarter of the median household disposable income in the early 1980s to 60 percent, skyrocketing the share of student loans in household debt and a consequence of this is dropouts.

Likewise, it seems, at first glance, to be a positive indicator that the country's expenditure on education as a percentage of GDP increased from 4.8 percent during the 1980s and 1990s on average to 5.3 percent in 2000s, by and large around the OECD average. However, the impact is yet to be seen. The National Educational Assessment Program illustrates that the country's performance in math and adult skills has been around the OECD average (the country's overall math, reading, and science performance nearly equaled the OECD average in 2006, but lagged the latter around 15 percent). A relevant indicator, patent applications of residents in the United States during the FEP constituted 94 percent of those in Japan, but this rate plummeted to 35 percent in the NLP (however, the applications of nonresidents were 1.5 and 4.5 times higher in the United States than those in Japan during the FEP and NLP, respectively [World Bank 2017]).

Another factor impacting the country's industrial performance is the decline in labor productivity. During the NLP, the US corporations treated employees as short-term liabilities rather than as long-term assets. In tandem with the shareholder model, employment relations in the contemporary US corporation have been structured on the basis of high labor market segmentation between two lines—innovative high-skilled and low-skilled production workers, de-unionization, individual wage contracts and unrestricted hiring and firing of employees, and the long and hard working conditions, particularly at the lower end of skill distribution (Hall and Soskice 2001; Amable 2000). Only a few US companies had employee ownership plans and initiated to bring employee views to senior management and to the board under mechanisms such as formal representation systems and board seats for employee or union representatives (Jacoby 2006: 49–50). Employers can take swift action and terminate an employee immediately citing underperformance or even illness without encountering any constraints such as a warning, severance pay, retirement, or sick leave (Steinmo 2010: 160).

As a result, during the period 1990–2013, the OECD and US employment protection index was 2.4 and 0.2 on an average, respectively (the OECD indicators of employment protection are synthetic indicators of the strictness of regulation on dismissals and the use of temporary contracts). A key consequence of an indecent IRs setting is the widening gap between labor productivity and real wages, as noted earlier. In addition, the changes in the earnings of low-skilled, medium-skilled, and high-skilled workers were minus 0.2, minus 0.4, and minus 0.8, respectively, as an average over the years 2004, 2008, and 2012. Similarly, while the OECD average earnings of the low-skilled and medium-skilled workers constitute 49 percent and 61 percent of the high-skilled ones, respectively, the same rates are 33 percent and 54 percent for the United States, respectively (OECD 2016b). As a result, the share of the top 20 percent in the income of labor groups turned 37 percent higher in 2000 than that in 1980 (Alvaredo et al. 2013). Apparently, this points to a sharp polarization of workers' earnings, particularly between the low- and high-skilled categories.

Industrial Governance

From the perspective of industrial policy choices, underlying the poor manufacturing and labor market performance in the United States is the lack of systemic governance between the president and the Congress, the federal and state governments, and between the public and private sectors in managing the country's industrial development, sectoral transitions, and education and skills strategies.

First, as elaborated below, the US presidents have a systemic power of coordination across the entire economy. However, Congress members should seriously focus on local demand to guarantee their reelection, primarily due to the nature of electoral system in the country. The discord between a few industrial strategies, driven by the presidents and the ad hoc interventions by members of the Congress on behalf of local industries, jeopardizes the pursuit of an organized and strategic industrial policy. Besides, this paradox has yet to be reconciled by the *formal* dialogues on industrial policy between the public and private sectors. For instance, the Manufacturing Initiative launched in March 2003 brought both sides together to discuss the significant loss of manufacturing jobs. The dialogue culminated with the establishment of a Manufacturers Council, which made a number of suggestions such as 'strengthening R&D credits, reducing healthcare and legal costs, investing in R&D and skills, and opening up of foreign markets'. However, the above summarized facts of the country's manufacturing performance well prove the ineffectiveness of such verbal guidance.

Second, the strong role of the states in regulating economic policy areas and industrial competition causes high degree of heterogeneity in industrial governance. One part of the problem is that the US economy has historically been an extensive and complex structure, with considerable heterogeneity of interests within sectors, making it quite difficult for firms to take collective action and develop effective associative structures for governing the sectors. Further, in a flexible labor market, employers avoid long-term investment in their employees' skills. This is attributable to the fact that arm's-length contraction on the basis of short-term market pricing requires firms to manage their labor costs in short periods and to preempt the cost of their potential employment by the other firms, apart from some of the research and growth-oriented high-tech sectors such as computers, biotechnology, and aerospace.

2.7   The Politics of Growth: The President and the Market

This section examines the political underpinnings of the country's G&D process from the FEP onward. There are inter alia three dynamics in the country's political system that can be regarded as PICs or NICs for G&D

in terms of the purpose for which they are deployed. These are a two-level executive order managed by the president holding coordinational and enforcive authority, a two-level electoral system, and political stability in terms of succession of power.

First, in the US model, there is a two-level executive system, the Cabinet and the Presidency. The Cabinet fulfills conventional executive functions ranging from transportation to justice and security. The president acts as a coordinator of last resort in charge of specifying and steering the direction of economic policy and growth. The Executive Office of the President (EOP) assists the president in enforcing these tasks. The EOP is responsible for coordinating major policy strategies ranging from macroeconomic to science and technology. There are four units in the EOP dealing with economic policy.

The Office of Management and Budget prepares the budget, administers its implementation, and inspects end-year realizations. The Council of Economic Advisers (CEA) advises the president on economic policy and provides policy analysis on major economic aggregates and developments such as growth, competition, and free trade. The Office of Science and Technology Policy coordinates policy development between the central and local public institutions, private sector, universities, and so on. The Office of the US Trade Representative specifies the international trade policy and resolves trade-related bureaucratic disputes. It is up to the president to reconcile the diverging perspectives of these four units in major economic policy issues. For this purpose, the National Economic Council (NEC) was founded in 1993 by President Clinton. The NEC coordinates internal-external economic policymaking for ensuring coherence of economic policy decisions and programs with the presidential objectives and goals and also monitors implementation of the president's policies (Ginsberg et al. 2015; Chaps. 3, 12, and 13; Corry 2011).

In this institutional setting, there are mainly two pillars that provide the US presidents with the power to sustain a systemic governance regime. The first is election by the public (a two-level election) rather than by the Congress, bestowing them a permanent power source beyond Congressional or intraparty skirmishes. The second is their ability to manage executive function by executive orders (Ginsberg et al. 2015: 509–510). Even though the Congress nominates executive functions to the Cabinet, the presidents have always tended to control these functions via executive orders. Thus, a two-level executive order might be suggested to be a PIC for the US model in the sense that the president holds a coordinative power to refrain political conflict of any kind from wreaking havoc on the economic order.

In particular, the president could eliminate coordinational failures among the federal executive departments in erecting and steering complementary linkages of macro- or microeconomic institutions (Thurber 2009). However, the same executive system might serve as a NIC in case the government avoids overtaking a coordinative role to strike a long-run trade-off between efficiency and equity. The US governments did so during the NLP on the basis of an inflation-obsessive economic policy, deregulatory financial and corporate governance, and a market-led industrial governance, resulting in the Great Recession, as elaborated above (Kamarck 2016; Weingast 1995).

Second, the two-level electoral system in the United States could also become a dynamic of both systemic governance and fragmentation. Underlying is the possibility that the electoral districts are relatively small and homogenous; the president and members of the Congress should pay attention to the expectations of their electorates. Specifically, they are expected to strike a trade-off between (1) the demands of ordinary citizens for egalitarian regulation in the face of inequality-creating consequences of a rent-seeking relationship between the Cabinet and the organized interest groups and (2) the private sector's demand for more deregulation for more investment and radical innovation. The nature of political system that requires such a trade-off underlied systemic governance during the FEP under the grim legacy of the Great Depression.

The second possibility is institutional fragmentation that would occur: first, the performance of candidates at the local level depends on their campaign budgets, the magnitude of which is determined by their relationship with local interest groups and national party organizations; and second, as individual voters are unable to follow jurisdictional processes, organized interest groups become influential in the decision-making processes at the Congress level (Sugrue 2003; Werner and Wilson 2010). Under the shadow of these two facts, the same electoral system had turned into a NIC in practice, causing economic inefficiency and inequity during the NLP.

During the NLP, political governance focused on sustaining incumbency by promoting financial support from financial and nonfinancial corporations at both the central and local levels to counteract institutionalization of deregulated economic, financial, and corporate governance. Within this context, high-income groups that participate in the 0.01 percent of the income brackets contributed more than 40 percent of total donation to political parties in 2012. As a corollary, less than half of the people whose yearly income is below US$ 15,000 voted for any party in the 2008 general elections, whereas more than four-fifths of people earning an average income above US$ 150,000 voted for any party in the same elections (Bonica et al. 2013: 112).

In the grip of growing financial industry donations, Democrats complied with the prerequisites of the neoliberal conjuncture, increasing Wall Street's economic and political clout in the party. As was seen during the Great Recession, this influence is as powerful as to prevent the Democrats to initiate *systemically* countercyclical action even after the housing bubble. What underlies this power is specific to the party's financial weakness compared to the Republican Party's budget and the declining propensity of low-income people to vote for any party. The Republicans have always had a surplus budget largely because of the donations made by corporations and the wealthy in consideration of the strategic alliance they have with the party (Hacker and Pierson 2010: 165–168).

Third, on the basis of a two-party tradition, the US political system has been stable in terms of succession of governments from the early nineteenth century onward. The US presidency has alternated between the Republicans and Democrats in most cases either after four- or eight-year periods. Importantly, the Republicans and Democrats succeeded each other after eight-year terms between 1953 and 1977 and between 1993 and 2016. Political stability is suggested to be a PIC that could prevent any potential inefficiency in the form of higher macroeconomic volatility and lower investments, as was the case during the full employment period. However, the positive role of political stability turns into negative in case if it is used to erect and consolidate fragmented governance. As witnessed during the NLP, fragmented governance resulted in lower growth, higher unemployment, and greater income inequality.

Efficiency or Equity: The Democrats Versus Republicans

Institutional settings during the FEP and the NLP regulated the policy strategies of both the Republicans and the Democrats. Yet, the US economy has always been a market-led one from the scratch. The full employment period was an era of transition during which the destructive consequences of the laissez-faire period were temporarily obscured to make the economy's basic pillars viable rather than sustainable, striking a *relative* trade-off between efficiency and equity. Therefore, as a revived form of laissez-faire capitalism, it emerges that neoliberalism rather than full employment constitutes the substance of the US political economy.

This can be observed from the fact that during the FEP, the Republicans had adopted policy strategies conducive to full employment on an ad hoc basis. The Democrats, however, adopted pro-neoliberal policies with the aim of maintaining popularity with a pro-market rhetoric, and being eligible for campaign finance as well as for the donations and votes of the rich whose electoral participation is quite high.

As can be seen in Fig. 2.5, during the periods they came to power between 1947–1952 and 1961–1968, the Democrats achieved higher growth and a lower rate of unemployment and inflation though the rates of government consumption and investment expenditures were extremely high (the impact of the Stagflation of the 1970s on inflation data during the Republican Party rule in the period 1969–1976 should be considered). The rate of corporate income tax was higher than during the periods between 1953–1960 and 1969–1976 when the Republicans held power. Above all, the annual change in real wages was nearly double of that during the Republicans' rule. Expectedly, as Bartels (2016: Chap. 2) concluded with the extension of Hibbs' analysis (1987) to the period 1948–2005, the top 20 percent received a lower and greater part of total income than that received by the bottom 40 percent during the rule of the Democrats and Republicans, respectively.

However, federal expenditures for social security and medicare for the period extending from 1946 to 1979 were the same for both Republicans and the Democrats, 2.7 percent of the country's GDP during the years they came to power, respectively, from 1948 to 1980. Further, the same expenditures were 6.3 and 6.9, respectively, when they came to power during the NLP. In the post-war period, despite a poor performance in growth, employment, and wages, the Republicans enforced significant social welfare reforms during Nixon's presidency (1969–1974). President Nixon offered major national welfare legislation by expanding the coverage of the social security system. He created a national food stamps program and transformed old-age assistance into a much larger and fully national Supplemental Security Income program. The Nixon administration adopted extensive regulatory discretion, ranging from creating the Environmental Protection Agency (1970), the Occupational Safety and Health Administration (1970), the Consumer Product Safety Commission, and the Mine Safety and Health Administration (1973) (Hacker and Pierson 2010: 70–72).

Interestingly, during the NLP, the Republicans and Democrats performed quite similar in terms of the annual rates of change in growth, real wages, and taxes on corporate income (Fig. 2.5). Furthermore, the Republicans seem to have pursued a much more expansionary fiscal policy, more than double that made by the Democrat governments. However, the defense budget rather than consumption or investment expenditures was responsible for this huge difference. Defense expenditures for the periods 1981–1992 and 2001–2008 were 3.4 percent and 4.5 percent, whereas nondefense expenditures were 2.4 percent and 3.2 percent, respectively.

The Democrats' nonactivist monetary policies during the Great Recession (2008–2015) might be attributed to the sizeable government indebtedness reaching 90 percent of GDP on average for the period from 2007 to 2015. Government expenditures, nonetheless, even during the Clinton presidency (1993–2000) lagged those during the Reagan and George W. Bush periods between 1981 and 1992.

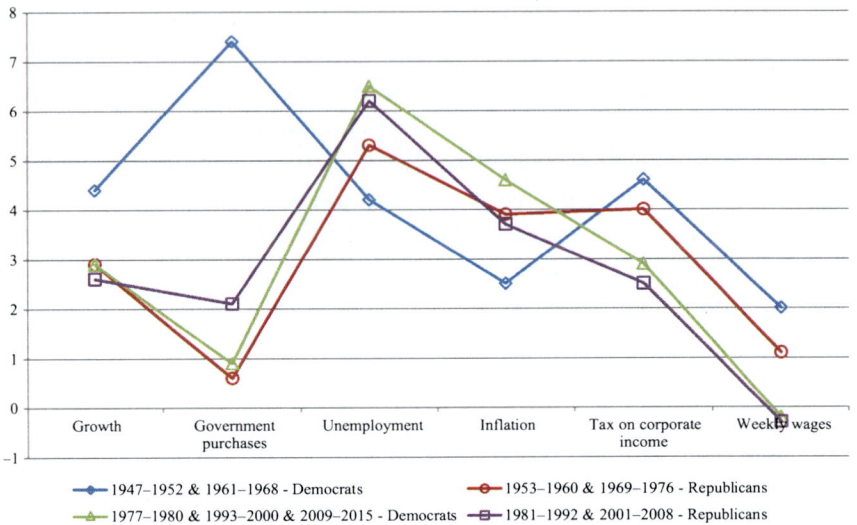

Fig. 2.5 Democrats' and Republicans' economic performance, 1947–2015. Source: US Bureau of Economic Analysis (2017); IMF (2017); U.S. President (1990, 2016)

In this context, concrete evidence for the fact that the Democrat Party left its countercyclical position in the NLP is that the party had enacted the Gramm-Leach-Bliley Act (GLBA) or the Financial Services Modernization Act of 1999 during Clinton's presidency in 1999. This Act primarily sought to repeal the ban imposed by the Glass-Steagall Act of 1933, which was enacted by President Roosevelt, another Democrat, on banking, securities, and insurance companies to act in any combination of investment bank, commercial bank, or as an insurance company (Bonica et al. 2013: 107). The lifting of this ban is of significance as it eradicated one of the key reasons that had caused the Great Depression.

In fact, the Dodd-Frank Act, enacted in 2010 during Obama's presidency, aimed to reduce the risk of financial crisis, for example, by redesigning financial governance such as the creation of a new public organization, the Financial Stability Oversight Council (FSOC), or the imposition of new requirements such as that for both parties of a derivative to clear it by arranging a clearing house for backing up their performance on the contract. However, this Act is essentially drawn on positive-sum reconciliation between the financial industry and the government without imposing binding regulations on shadow banking and any sanction on the government failure in overtaking regulatory discretion, without eliminating over-complexity in the financial system and the potential challenges caused by banks that are *too-big-to-fail*.

Instead, controversially, due to the government's partnership with the largest Wall Street banks, the Act requires the government to preclude the failure of two groups of financial institutions: banks with a minimum of US$ 50 billion in assets and nonbank financial institutions classified by the FSOC as pivotal for the financial system. Apparently, such a treatment will provide these institutions with a regulation-induced competitive power and a permanent incentive to take excessive risks with a lower level of borrowing cost. Most importantly, the Act does not make any regulation that inspires or entails the financial sector to perform its job of funding productive sectors, by any government- or Fed-led incentives (Stiglitz 2016: 20; Kane 2012; Kim and Muldoon 2015: 96–97).

2.8   Conclusion: Institutional Trap in the Period 2007–2017

Between 2009 and 2012, the US government assumed discretionary activism with a fiscal stimulus of 1.4 trillion dollars when combined with the automatic stabilizers. The basic means of this activism were individual tax cuts and business tax incentives, aid to directly impacted individuals and state fiscal relief, and public investment in infrastructure, education, job training, energy, and health information technology (U.S. President 2017: 34).

In addition to reducing the federal funds rate close to zero by the end of 2008, the Fed also aims to reduce the long-term interest rate mainly through asset purchases, known as quantitative easing, and purchasing long-term debt instruments, such as mortgage-backed securities and US treasury securities. Indeed, as of May 2017, the Fed's assets comprised 55 percent government securities and 40 percent mortgage-backed securities.

In doing so, the Fed's balance sheet increased from 872 billion dollars in 2007 to nearly 4.5 trillion dollars by May 2017, remaining largely stagnant from 2014 onward with the announcement of the *normalization of monetary policy* in September 2014. This policy aims to reduce the Fed's securities holdings and gradually raise its target range for the federal funds rate and other short-term interest rates to more normal levels (Fed 2017b).

In terms of the consequences of these policy choices, the 2017 Economic Report of the President (ERP) emphasizes two main points. The first is that 'the response of the Federal Government to the crisis averted a sharper and more prolonged downturn and put the US economy back on a path to growth.' While it is true that growth recovered to 2 percent and unemployment receded to 5 percent in 2016, there are two main problems with this first point.

The first is that the Report does not concentrate on US economic performance during and after the housing bubble, namely, throughout the period 2007–2017, but rather concentrates on the recent recovery (a periodic analysis is of significance for explaining the durability of the so-called recovery). As Table 2.1 illustrates, this period has been characterized by low inflation and high unemployment. An extremely low level of growth (1.3 percent on average) was achieved with zero contribution from the government and private sector even though the profitability in the nonfinancial sector rose from 5 percent in the NLP to 7 percent and that real lending interest rates declined by more than 100 percent. Instead of investing, the business sector increased its savings from 12.3 percent in the NLP to 13.8 percent in the period 2007–2015 as well as distributed the returns of its earnings to shareholders in the form of dividends and share buybacks (Gruber and Kamin 2015).

As a result, the contribution of private investment under the negative multiplier impact of budgetary austerity declined to zero in the period 2007–2015 from an average of 0.7 in the NLP. (Paradoxically, despite almost doubling its debt stock, the financial sector's value added to GDP continues growing with a trivial decline in its share of corporate profits; see Table 2.3.) In a similar vein, the value added of the manufacturing sector to GDP declined by more than one-quarter on average from that in the

NLP along with a tremendous increase in current account deficits (3 percent of GDP). The rate of capacity utilization in the manufacturing sector changed by minus 0.2 percent on average in the period 2007–2015.

Overall, aggregate demand fell dramatically in this period, and a low rate of growth was helped by the contribution of debt-financed consumption expenditure (1.1 percent). And the output gap reached minus 2.6 percent in the period 2007–2016 (Congressional Budget Office 2017). Furthermore, this high rate is possible only with the downward revision of real potential GDP rates. (Potential output was earlier projected to grow at an average rate of 2.9 percent between 2007 and 2016 [CBO 2006: 48]. This rate has now been revised to 1.4 percent [CBO 2017].)

The second problem in the Report's positive projection of growth is that the so-called *recovery* has been a debt-financed one, with a more than overall 40 percent increase in the indebtedness of the government, households, and businesses on average (see Table 2.1) and a more than fivefold increase in the Fed's balance sheet between 2008 and 2016. This second reason has manifested itself in a gradual process of rising budgetary austerity from 2010 and the Fed's decision to normalize monetary policy. Thus, the contribution of government expenditure to growth declined to minus 0.2 percent in 2010–2015 from 0.5 percent in 2007–2009. In addition, the Fed's balance sheet remained largely constant in 2015 and 2016 despite the announcement of its policy normalization target in September 2014.

As OECD (2016a: 19) notes, in such an overloaded fiscal and monetary setting, the scope for responding to adverse shocks has become restrained. If the Fed was to increase interest rates, this could jeopardize the country's already mediocre economic growth. In this sense, by underlying the stickiness of the Fed's overloaded balance sheet with a zero lower bound strategy, 'the risks of stagnation exceed those of overheating, and quite likely the risks of too little credit growth exceed of those too much credit growth' (Summers 2015: 64). Moreover, as observed with rising austeritarianism, fiscal policy is far from assuming a more discretionary role by fostering growth with a level of debt reaching 106 percent of GDP in 2016.

The second point that the 2017 ERP emphasizes is that the tax reforms during Obama's presidency helped the income distribution. However, US Census Bureau statistics on the distribution of aggregate income and rate of change in marginal income tax for the top decile, documented in Table 2.2, do not substantiate this argument. The Gini coefficient before taxes jumped to 0.47 during the GRP on average from 0.44 in the NLP and marginal income tax for the top decile was further reduced at a rate of 16.2 percent. According to OECD estimations, the Gini coefficient after taxes for the period 2007–2015 increased to 0.38 on an average from 0.36 in the period 1993–2006.

In a similar vein, the rates of change in labor productivity and in real hourly wages were 1.25 percent and 0.6 percent, respectively, in the period 2007–2015. Furthermore, the Report (U.S. President 2017: 43) itself notes that 'A number of decades-long trends that preceded the crisis—rising inequality, insufficient health insurance coverage, high health care costs, and growing costs for higher education—still remained, preventing middle-class Americans from seeing gains in their incomes, economic security, and standards of living.'

Thus, this expansionary economic policy has come no closer to removing the country from the enduring stagnation. A key indicator in this regard is that total factor productivity, the basic indicator of innovative dynamism, has remained nearly threefold less than that in the NLP. Total factor productivity has been shown to be the preferred alternative for reducing the pressure on the overloaded balance sheets of the US government and the Fed; however, it has even been sluggish in frontier sectors such as ICT and pharmaceuticals (GGDC 2017). Concerning the other indicators of institutional performance, the situation is not bright either. In particular, the private investment trend in the GRP and the GSNP illustrates that corporate governance has yet to refocus on investment and productivity rather than on short-term gains and shareholder value.

Overall, the country has been stuck in the institutional trap of low growth, high unemployment, and slackening industrial progress over the past decade (the GRP of 2007–2009 and the GSNP of 2010–2017). In institutional terms, this trap makes sense since successive US governments have yet to turn the country's NICs-dominated model in the grip of embedded institutional fragmentation into a PICs-dominated one by enforcing systemic change. Instead, they have embarked on harnessing the crisis through nonsystemic reforms such as the Dodd-Frank Act. How a PICs-dominated systemic governance might be adopted in the American context and what types of institutional changes are required (major questions in themselves) should apparently be the subject matter of further research.

References

Alvaredo, F., Atkinson, A. B., Piketty, T., & Saez, E. (2013). The Top One Percent in International and Historical Perspective. *Journal of Economic Perspectives, 27*(3), 1–21.

Amable, B. (2000). Institutional Complementarity and Diversity of Social Systems of Innovation and Production. *Review of International Political Economy, 7*(4), 645–687.

Arrighi, G. (1994). *The Long Twentieth Century: Money, Power, and the Origins of Our Times*. London: Verso.

Baily, M. N., & Bosworth, B. P. (2014). US Manufacturing: Understanding Its Past and Its Potential Future. *Journal of Economic Perspectives, 28*(1), 3–26.

Bairoch, P. (1993). *Economics and the World History: Myths and Paradoxes*. Chicago: Chicago University Press.

Bakir, E., & Campbell, A. (2013). The Financial Rate of Profit: What Is It, and How Has It Behaved in the United States? *Review of Radical Political Economics, 45*(3), 295–304.

Bartels, L. M. (2016). *Unequal Democracy: The Political Economy of the New Gilded Age*. Princeton: Princeton University Press.

Bonica, A., McCarty, N., Poole, K. T., & Rosenthal, H. (2013). Why Hasn't Democracy Slowed Rising Inequality. *Journal of Economic Perspectives, 27*(3), 103–124.

Bureau of Economic Analysis. (2017). *National Accounts*. Retrieved February 5, 2017, from https://bea.gov/index.htm

Bureau of Labor Statistics. (2017a). *Major Sector Data*. Retrieved April 8, 2017, from https://www.bls.gov/lpc/#tables

Bureau of Labor Statistics. (2017b). *Occupational Employment Statistics*. Retrieved April 8, 2017, from https://www.bls.gov/oes/current/naics3_999000.htm

Campbell, J. L. (2011). The US Financial Crisis: Lessons for Theories of Institutional Complementarity. *Socio-Economic Review, 9*(2), 211–234.

Carmassi, J., Gros, D., & Micossi, S. (2009). Global Financial Crisis: Causes and Cures. *Journal of Common Market Studies, 47*(5), 977–996.

Congressional Budget Office (CBO). (2006). *The Budget and Economic Outlook: Fiscal Years 2007 to 2016.* Washington, DC: United States Congress.

Congressional Budget Office (CBO). (2017). *Potential Output and Underlying Data.* Retrieved May 17, 2017, from https://www.cbo.gov/about/products/budget-economic-data#6

Corry, D. (2011). Power at the Centre: Is the National Economic Council a Model for a New Way of Organizing Things. *Political Quarterly, 82*(3), 459–468.

Council of Economic Advisers (CEA). (2016). *Benefits of Competition and Indicators of Market Power.* Retrieved February 8, 2017, from https://obamawhitehouse.archives.gov/sites/default/files/page/files/20160414_cea_competition_issue_brief.pdf

Dore, R. (2002). Stock Market Capitalism and Its Diffusion. *New Political Economy, 7*(1), 115–121.

Edwards, L., & Lawrence, R. Z. (2013). *Rising Tide: Is Growth in Emerging Economies Good for the United States.* Washington, DC: Peterson Institute for International Economics.

Federal Reserve System (Fed). (2017a). *Enhanced Financial Accounts.* Retrieved April 26, 2017, from https://www.federalreserve.gov/datadownload/Choose.aspx?rel=Z.1

Federal Reserve System (Fed). (2017b). *Quarterly Report on Federal Reserve Balance Sheet Developments—May 2017.* Retrieved April 26, 2017, from https://www.federalreserve.gov/monetarypolicy/quarterly-balance-sheet-developments-report.htm

Financial Crisis Inquiry Commission (FCIC). (2011). *Financial Crisis Inquiry Report.* Submitted to the US Congress in January 2011, Washington, DC.

Ginsberg, B., Theodore, J. L., Weir, M., Tolbert, C. J., & Spitzer, R. (2015). *We the People: An Introduction to American Politics* (10th ed.). New York: W.W. Norton & Company.

Golub, S., Kaya, A., & Reay, M. (2015). What Were They Thinking? The Federal Reserve in the Run-up-to the 2008 Financial Crisis. *Review of International Political Economy, 22*(4), 657–692.

Gordon, R. (2012). *Is U.S. Economic Growth Over? Faltering Innovation Confronts the Six Headwinds.* NBER Working Paper 18135. Retrieved April 8, 2017, from http://www.nber.org/papers/w18315.pdf

Groningen Growth and Development Centre (GGDC). (2017). *PENN World Tables 9.0*. Retrieved October 11, 2016, from http://www.rug.nl/ggdc/productivity/pwt/

Gruber, J. W., & Kamin, S. B. (2015). *The Corporate Saving Glut in the Aftermath of the Global Financial Crisis*. FRB International Finance Discussions Papers 1150. Retrieved May 4, 2017, from https://papers.ssrn.com/sol3/papers.cfm?abstract_id=2686986

Hacker, J. S., & Pierson, P. (2010). *Winner-Take-All Politics*. New York: Simon and Schuster.

Hakkio, S. (2013). *The Great Moderation, 1982–2007*. Retrieved May 12, 2017, from https://www.federalreservehistory.org/essays/great_moderation

Hall, P., & Soskice, D. (2001). *Varieties of Capitalism: The Institutional Bases of Comparative Advantage*. Oxford: Oxford University Press.

Hibbs, D. (1987). *The American Political Economy: Macroeconomics and Electoral Politics*. Cambridge, MA: Harvard University Press.

Hilt, E. (2014). *History of American Corporate Governance: Law, Institutions, and Politics*. NBER Working Paper 20356. Retrieved March 7, 2017, from http://www.nber.org/papers/w20356

Hirst, P., & Zeitlin, J. (1991). Flexible Specialization Versus Post-Fordism: Theory, Evidence and Policy Implications. *Economy and Society, 20*(1), 2–56.

Hollingsworth, J. R. (1999). The Logic of Coordinating American Manufacturing Sectors. In J. L. Campbell, J. R. Hollingsworth, & L. N. Lindberg (Eds.), *The Governance of American Economy* (pp. 35–73). Cambridge: Cambridge University Press.

Holstrom, B., & Kaplan, S. N. (2001). Corporate Governance and Merger Activity in the United States: Making Sense of the 1980s and 1990s. *Journal of Economic Perspectives, 15*(2), 121–144.

IMF. (2017). *Financial Statistics*. Retrieved April 7, 2017, from http://data.imf.org/?sk=5477AD05-460D-4C91-9690-11E99B1ED935&sId=1390030341854

Jackson, G. (2010). *Understanding Corporate Governance in the United States: A Historical and Theoretical Reassessment*. Hans Böckler Stiftung, Arbeitspapier 223. Retrieved April 15, 2017, from http://www.boeckler.de/pdf/p_arbp_223.pdf

Jacoby, S. M. (2006). Corporate Governance and Employees in the United States. In H. Gospel & A. Pendleton (Eds.), *Corporate Governance and Labor Management: An International Comparison* (pp. 33–59). Oxford: Oxford University Press.

Kamarck, E. C. (2016). *Why Presidents Fail and How They Can Succeed Again*. Washington, DC: Brookings Institution Press.

Kane, E. J. (2012). Missing Element in US Financial System: A Kübler-Ross Interpretation of the Inadequacy of the Dodd-Frank Act. *Journal of Banking & Finance, 36,* 654–661.

Keller, M. R., & Block, F. (2011). Do As I Say, or As I Do? US Innovation and Industrial Policy Since the 1980s. In J. Felipe (Ed.), *Development and Modern Industrial Policy in Practice* (pp. 219–246). Cheltenham: Edward Elgar.

Kim, S. H., & Muldoon, C. (2015). The Dodd-Frank Wall Street Reform and Consumer Protection Act: Accomplishments and Shortcomings. *Journal of Applied Business and Economics, 17*(3), 92–107.

Kirkpatrick, G. (2009). *Corporate Governance Lessons from the Financial Crisis.* Paris: OECD.

Konings, M. (2011). *The Development of American Finance.* Cambridge: Cambridge University Press.

Kozul-Wright, R. (1995). The Myth of Anglo-Saxon Capitalism: Reconstructing the History of the American State. In H. Chang & R. Rowthorn (Eds.), *The Role of the State in Economic Change* (pp. 82–113). Oxford: Oxford University Press.

Krippner, G. R. (2005). The Financialization of the American Economy. *Socio-Economic Review, 3,* 173–208.

Law, M., & Kim, S. (2011). Historical and Comparative Perspectives on the Regulatory State. In D. Levi-Faur (Ed.), *Handbook on the Politics of Regulation* (pp. 113–128). Cheltenham: Edward Elgar.

Lazonick, W. (2005). Corporate Restructuring. In S. Ackroyd & R. Batt (Eds.), *The Oxford Handbook of Work and Organization* (pp. 577–601). Oxford: Oxford University Press.

Meulendyke, A. (1998). *U.S. Monetary Policy and Financial Markets.* Federal Reserve Bank of New York. Retrieved May 8, 2017, from https://research. stlouisfed.org/aggreg/meulendyke.pdf

Nester, W. R. (1998). *A Short History of American Industrial Policies.* Basingstoke: Macmillan.

New York Times (NYT). (2008, October 23). *Greenspan Concedes Error on Regulation.* Retrieved November 4, 2017, from http://www.nytimes.com/2008/10/24/business/economy/24panel.html

OECD. (2009). *Corporate Governance and the Financial Crisis.* Paris: OECD.

OECD. (2014). *All on Board: Making Inclusive Growth Happen.* Paris: OECD.

OECD. (2016a). *OECD Economic Surveys: United States.* Paris: OECD.

OECD. (2016b). *Educational Statistics.* Retrieved February 17, 2016, from http://www.oecd.org/education/

Orhangazi, Ö. (2008). *Financialization and the US Economy*. Cheltenham: Edward Elgar.

Palley, T. (2012). *From Financial Crisis to Stagnation: The Destruction of Shared Prosperity and the Role of Economics*. Cambridge: Cambridge University Press.

Palley, T. (2013). *Financialization: The Economics of Finance Capital Domination*. Basingstoke: Palgrave Macmillan.

Pierce, J. R., & Schott, P. K. (2014). *The Surprisingly Swift Decline of U.S. Manufacturing Employment*. FRB Finance and Economics Discussion Series 2014-04. Retrieved July 8, 2017, from https://www.federalreserve.gov/pubs/feds/2014/201404/201404pap.pdf

Piketty, T. (2013). *Capital in the Twenty-First Century* (A. Goldhammer, Trans.). Cambridge, MA: Belknap Press.

Saez, E., & Piketty, T. (2003). Income Inequality in the United States, 1913–1998. *Quarterly Journal of Economics, 118*(1), 1–41.

Schiler, R. J. (2009). *Irrational Exuberance* (3rd ed.). Princeton: Princeton University Press. Retrieved June 4, 2017, from http://www.econ.yale.edu/~shiller/data.htm

Sorenson, D. P., & Miller, S. E. (2017). Financial Accounting Standards and the Reform of Corporate Governance in the United States and in Italy. *Corporate Governance: The International Journal of Business in Society, 17*(1), 77–88.

Steinmo, S. (2010). *The Evolution of Modern States: Sweden, Japan, and the United States*. Cambridge: Cambridge University Press.

Stiglitz, J. (2013). *The Price of Inequality: How Today's Divided Society Endangers Our Future*. New York: W. W. Norton & Company.

Stiglitz, J. (2016). *Rewriting the Rules of the American Economy: An Agenda for Growth and Shared Prosperity*. New York: W.W. Norton & Company.

Sugrue, T. J. (2003). All Politics Is Local: The Persistence of Localism in Twentieth America. In M. Jacobs, W. Novak, & J. Zelizer (Eds.), *The Democratic Experiment: New Directions in American Political History* (pp. 301–326). Princeton: Princeton University Press.

Summers, L. S. (2015). Demand Side Secular Stagnation. *American Economic Review, 105*(5), 60–65.

Sylla, R. (2007). Reversing Financial Reversals: Government and the Financial System Since 1789. In P. V. Fishback (Ed.), *Government and the American Economy* (pp. 117–147). Chicago: Chicago University Press.

Thelen, K. (2014). *Varieties of Liberalization and the New Politics of Social Solidarity*. New York, NY: Cambridge University Press.

Thurber, J. A. (2009). An Introduction to Presidential-Congressional Rivalry. In J. A. Thurber & J. Tama (Eds.), *Rivals for Power: Presidential-Congressional Relations* (4th ed., pp. 1–36). Lanham: Rowman & Littlefield Publishers.

U.S. Census Bureau. (2017). *Current Population Survey, Annual Social and Economic Supplements*. Retrieved April 7, 2017, from https://www2.census.gov/programs-surveys/cps/tables/time-series/historical-income households/h04.xls

U.S. President. (1990). *Economic Report of the President*. Washington, DC: Government Printing Office.

U.S. President. (2016). *Economic Report of the President*. Washington, DC: Government Printing Office.

U.S. President. (2017). *Economic Report of the President*. Washington, DC: Government Printing Office.

Vietor, R. H. K. (2000). Government Regulation of Business. In S. L. Engerman & R. E. Gallman (Eds.), *Cambridge History of American Economy: The Twentieth Century* (Vol. III, pp. 969–1012). Cambridge: Cambridge University Press.

Vitols, S. (2001). The Origins of Bank-Based and Market-Based Financial Systems: Germany, Japan, and the United States. In W. Streeck & K. Yamamura (Eds.), *Origins of Nonliberal Capitalism: Germany and Japan in Comparison* (pp. 171–199). Ithaca: Cornell University Press.

Wade, R. (2012). Return of Industrial Policy. *International Review of Applied Economics, 26*(2), 223–239.

Wade, R. (2014). The Paradox of US Industrial Policy: The Developmental State in Disguise. In J. M. Salazar-Xirinachs, I. Nübler, & R. Kozul-Wright (Eds.), *Transforming Economies: Making Industrial Policy Work for Growth, Jobs, and Development* (pp. 379–400). Geneva: International Labor Organization.

Walton, G. M., & Rockoff, H. (2014). *History of the American Economy* (12th ed.). South-Western: Cengage Learning.

Weingast, B. R. (1995). The Economic Role of Political Institutions: Market-Preserving Federalism and Economic Development. *The Journal of Law, Economics & Organization, 11*(1), 1–31.

Werner, T., & Wilson, G. (2010). Business Representation in Washington, DC. In D. Coen, W. Grant, & G. Wilson (Eds.), *Business and Government* (pp. 261–284). Oxford: Oxford University Press.

World Bank. (2017). *World Development Indicators*. Retrieved March 4, 2017, from http://databank.worldbank.org/data/reports.aspx?source=world-development-indicators

3

Rise and Fall of the State-Led Model: South Korea

Abstract South Korea is a developed country that first achieved a miracle under a state-led model but then failed in sustaining that performance. In this chapter, the country's G&D performance has been examined mainly in four periods: 1961–1979, 1980–1996, 1997–2007, and 2008–2015. Using the analytic frame suggested in Chap. 1, this chapter concludes that the root cause of the South Korea's impressive and faltering performance of G&D in the first and the subsequent two periods, respectively, has been the establishment of an intrinsic model of systemic governance and the fragmentation of its institutional complementarities, respectively. And this process of fragmentation throughout nearly three decades has ended up with an institutional trap in the last period.

Keywords South Korea • Growth • Development • Institutions • Complementarity • Governance

© The Author(s) 2018
T. Akan, *The Complementary Roots of Growth and Development*,
https://doi.org/10.1007/978-3-319-68932-6_3

3.1 Introduction

South Korea features a model that first achieved a miracle but then failed to sustain the performance. The country's G&D process can be divided into four periods, shown in the Fig. 3.1. The four periods can be aggregated into the first between 1961 and 1979, and the subsequent three periods from the 1980s onward. The country's economic governance strategy was shifted from liberal protectionism in the first period to neo-liberal deregulation beginning in the early 1980s, specifically from the early 1990s onward.

The country's high-growth trend continued during the first and second periods, albeit unevenly, on an average of 9 percent. Subsequently, growth plummeted to 5 percent and 3 percent during the third and fourth periods, respectively. As the major indicator of industrial sophistication, the value added of a manufacturing sector to GDP rose steadily to 30 percent in the fourth period from 19 percent in the first period. The highest increase was seen in the high-value-added manufactures from 20 percent in the second to 30 percent in the third period, although declining to 27 percent in the last (fourth) period. The Gini coefficient declined from 0.39 in 1980 to 0.24 in 1992, but rose gradually to 0.31 in 2007 and remained steady at that level until 2016.

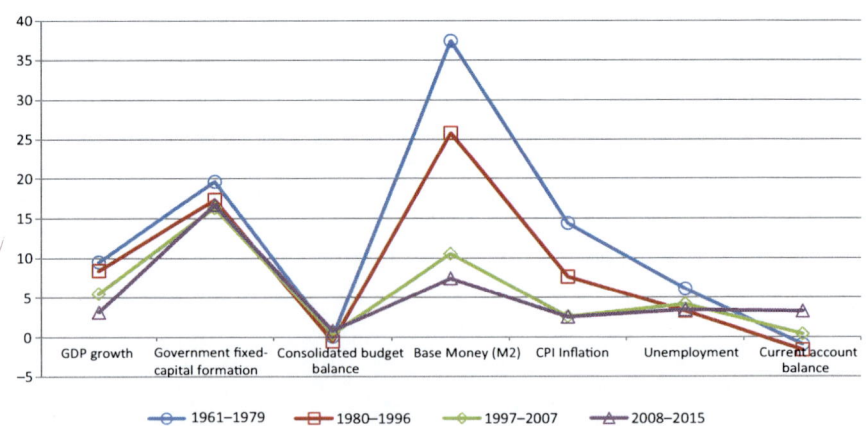

Fig. 3.1 Basic indicators of South Korean economy, 1961–2015. Source: IMF (2017); World Bank (2017); Song (1990: 60–61)

As a result, South Korea failed to sustain economic growth and reduce income inequality during the third and fourth periods. Industrial sophistication improved in the third period, but the trend also could not be sustained in the last period. Essentially, in this chapter, it is suggested that the fundamental cause of the country's impressive and faltering performances of G&D in the first and the subsequent two periods was the establishment of an intrinsic model of systemic governance and fragmentation of the country's institutional stock in the second and third periods, respectively. Further, this process of fragmentation through nearly three decades culminated in an institutional trap during the fourth period. This analysis will be from a complementary theoretical perspective.

The chapter has been organized into two sections. The first section examines South Korea's G&D performance during the above-noted four periods with reference to economic policy and financial and corporate governance. The section begins with an analysis of the first period under the framework of *authoritarian entrepreneurship* as a mode of systemic governance proper to the country. Next, the section investigates the beginning and embedding of institutional fragmentation and drift during the second and third periods. Finally, the discussion focuses on the fourth period as a specific stage of institutional trap between developmentalism, deregulation, and maturation.

The second section of the chapter offers a detailed insight into the industrial, political, and socioeconomic foundations of the country's G&D experience in terms of deteriorating manufacturing performance under an erratic industrial policy, the impact of flawed political democratization on overall institutional fragmentation, and rising inequality in the process of unmatched economic and political development. The chapter concludes with a complete analysis of the country's G&D.

3.2   The Systemic Governance of Economic Development in South Korea, 1961–1979

In the early 1950s, Korea hardly had a promising future in G&D, largely due to the emerging chaos and vacuum created at the end of the Japan's colonization of 36 years, the arbitrary division of the country into North and South, and the ensuing civil war. What worsened the plight of the country was the incumbent predatory state governance under Syngman Rhee from 1948 to 1960.

The Syngman Rhee regime established a rent-based social system for allocating subsidies, financial credit, and import licenses as well as in supplementing bureaucrats' salaries through corruption, thereby failing to achieve sustained economic growth. Albeit showing remarkable diplomatic skills in foreign relations and a democratic constitution of 1948, the regime failed in erecting a cross-class coalition and in managing rising conflict with the opposition parties, military, labor unions, and civil society groups such as church organizations. Underlying the Rhee regime was the US military and financial support to the country so that it resists a communist threat (nearly 60 percent of the country's budget comprised of US funds). Finally, following an electoral fraud during the 1960 elections, students revolted and forced Rhee to resign in an uprising called the April Revolution.

Albeit receiving 82 percent of total votes in the 1960 elections, the Democratic Party of Korea also could not ensure public order and pacify the continuing social strife. In May 1961, General Park Chung-hee engineered a coup d'état and seized power. In 1963, the military restored parliamentary order, but Park Chung-hee's dictatorial regime continued de facto until his assassination in October 1979. As the prime institution executing the Korean War of 1950–1953, the army was then the most powerful and professional institution countervailing the Rhee administration to cause a fit between its members.

Thus, the civil administration's failure to maintain public order and ensure economic prosperity, paradoxically, legitimized the dictatorial rule in the country for the entire period between the 1960s and the 1970s (Mo and Weingast 2013: 50–62). President Park declared martial law, dissolved all the political parties and the National Assembly, censored the press, banned all public demonstrations, and issued anti-communist laws conferring on the state the power to arrest and convict opponents. He remained powerful until his assassination by the head of the Korean intelligence agency on 26 October 1979 owing to a disagreement on how to placate growing public unrest.

As noted in Chap. 1, South Korea adopted a G&D model called *authoritarian entrepreneurship*, the institutional pillars of which were delineated earlier. In this section, these pillars will be examined comprehensively.

During the first period of its G&D process, South Korea achieved the highest average growth of 9.5 percent in its history under state intervention, even though the rate of unemployment was also the highest, 6 percent on an average, among the four periods under consideration. During this period, the monetary base was expanded annually by more than 30 percent on an average to finance government deficits, support industrial policies, and maintain a negative real lending interest rate in the 1970s, which resulted in 14 percent average inflation during the period. In addition, the average of foreign debt per annum was around 7 percent for the entire period, in particular 10 percent in the 1970s. And the current account deficit reached chronic rates at the end of the period due to the dependence on imported machinery and oil.

However, South Korea achieved a miraculous growth rate despite the unfavorable macroeconomic environment as it succeeded in establishing its G&D model striking a complementary trade-off between political authoritarianism, protectionist liberalism, economic progressiveness, and shared growth.

In terms of state-market nexus, governance councils, particularly the Korea's Economic Planning Board, enabled this complementarity through the formulation and implementation of consensus-based policy choices. The Board consisted of state bureaucrats, representatives of business and labor, academia, and so on. It functioned as a platform of credible commitment where governments delivered their promises made to businesses and nonelites, contributed to the reduction of transaction costs and information asymmetries in addition to monitoring a dynamic process of industrial transformation, thereby fostering economic growth and prosperity (Ahrens 2002: 220). For example, monthly meetings were held between bureaucrats and the exporting (public or private) enterprises to monitor or revise the export targets set at the industry, product, and firm levels. The bureaucrats were directly responsible for the attainment of these export targets by developing close ties with the exporting enterprises

(Shin and Chang 2003: 7–33). Besides including these positive complementary inputs in the country's G&D, the Board also played a legitimizing role for state authoritarianism.

South Korea's bureaucracy had long-term career prospects and earned a salary, benefits, and allowance much closer to that in the private sector, essentially on the basis of meritocratic recruitment and performance-based promotion. This bureaucratic structure could not fully eliminate, but succeeded in preventing corruption to hold sway over the entire system. Against this backdrop, and in a strong hierarchical setting, the bureaucracy managed to calibrate the delicate balance between economic productivity, wealth sharing, and the prevention of social conflict with their entrepreneurial responsibilities, thereby contributing toward the sustenance of *autocratic efficiency*.

Led by a bureaucratic strata empowered with a system-wide controlling authority, the Korean state governed the internal-external evolution of industrial sectors through protective and deregulatory measures by applying high tariff and quantitative restrictions as well as implicit, explicit, and selective subsidies to specific sectors on the basis of performance criteria. The state also directed transnational corporations into high-value-added sectors, conditioned technology, and skill transfer of local firms and discouraged the former's entry into the sectors where the latter were strong (foreign direct investment [FDI] was limited to 1 percent between 1971 and 1980). The state intervened even in the rationalization of firm structures either merging them with an international firm or dividing them into two or more entities (Kong 2012: 244).

Technological advancement served as the core complementarity of entrepreneurship under an authoritarian regime in South Korea. The country subsidized technology imports and transfer costs of patent rights. Technology import fees tax was deductible; income from technological consulting tax exempt and foreign engineers was exempt from income tax. When required, the public sector invested in several heavy and high-technology sectors where private sector investment was not viable. Two factors made this public strategy feasible. First, the country's education system was structured to train a qualified stock of engineers to take up the technical responsibility of this entrepreneurship as well as to adopt and reengineer foreign technologies (Di Maio 2009: 111–115), and second, cooperation between state-owned banks and state enterprises in steering the linkage between production and finance.

The state development banks of South Korea reserved special funds to finance technological development and innovation by extending long-term subsidized and direct credit to the exporting firms. Under a fixed-exchange rate regime and the state's strategic protectionism, this financial support increased the predictability of institutional environment and contributed to the stability of industrial investment in high-tech sectors, as in the coordinated market economies of Europe. Such a production-finance nexus also made it possible to prevent the breakdown of financial cycles between savings accounts in development banks and investment credit into specific sectors, forming an autocratic stakeholder model. Similarly, through foreign exchange control, the state confined the use of foreign exchange only to the central bank and designated commercial banks, aimed at preventing manipulative initiatives such as currency speculation and unproductive investments abroad (Lee 1992).

The dynamic complementarity between the nonfinancial business sector and the state functioned through a credible commitment to the country's growth-driven institutional equilibria. For this purpose, *chaebols*—a model of family-owned large private conglomerates—originated in the 1970s to initiate costly and risky investment in complex technologies and develop these technologies further through their own research and development activities as well as to create robust brand names and set up distribution channels (Kim and Park 2011). *Chaebols* thrived under the state's organizing guidance with high reliance on debt financing, a horizontal diversified structure, and a centralized and hierarchical decision-making process.

Policy loans and state guarantees were the driving force behind *chaebols* to venture into high-risk competitive investment, given the performance criteria that consisted of increasing output and/or export levels. Besides, the organizational and financial structures of *chaebols* were managed by insiders or founder families and intragroup shareholders, which continued until 1998, and made it possible to conduct *strong managerialism* to manage potential negative consequences of these risky investments. What tied corporate governance, in this respect, to wider developmental goals was *chaebols'* conformance to macroeconomic policy goals in view of state's power to make changes in the discount rate or in concessional credit rates between sectors, which could considerably alter resource allocation. The state also held the power to divide bankrupt *chaebols* and facilitate a takeover when their performance lagged. Such corporate governance paved the way for complementary learning and commitment between the state, corporate owners/managers, labor, and financial capital (Chang 1996: 123; Kang 2010: 534).

On the other hand, in broad strokes, South Korea's socioeconomic strategy from 1961 to 1979 can be dubbed *authoritarian egalitarianism* in the sense that the state's core strategy was to control society and use egalitarian measures as the basic means to exercise the so-called control. The main policy instruments of this strategy were the state's large investment in universal education and asset transfers to the public. In addition to developing human resource infrastructure for the economic transformation of the capital- and technology-intensive industries, these two policy instruments also reinforced one of the basic components of the model: relatively equitable distribution of career opportunities and wealth as the buffer mechanism for social uprisings and the source of higher savings. The Gini coefficient reduced from 0.44 in 1960 to 0.39 in 1980 after declining to 0.33 in 1970.

As the basic means of socioeconomic control, organized labor was harshly suppressed and kept under strict control through legal arrangements that compelled firm- and industry-level unions to affiliate with only one union, the Federation of Korean Trade Unions (minimum wage was not adopted until 1986). Trade union density averaged 13 percent during the period 1960–1979 and there were only 21 worker strikes in the period 1969–1973, but this rate soared to 70 per year between 1974 and 1979 (Kim 2010a: 100–105). However, in order to appease the regime's systemic repression, a few protective measures were adopted ranging from the creation of a system of national industrial accident insurance, legal sanctioning of the priority of wage claims over creditors in case of bankruptcy, and active promotion of firm-level social welfare schemes, even against the *chaebols'* resistance (Kang 2010: 531–532). The outcome of these mixed blessings resulted in an 11.3 percent real wage growth in the face of a 7.1 percent increase in labor productivity per capita in the manufacturing sector.

3.3   Primordial Institutional Fragmentation of the Korean Model, 1980–1996

During the period 1980–1996, the country passed through a crisis of reorganization between the remnants of entrepreneurship during an authoritarian regime and the rising demand for economic and political democracy. South Korea adopted a democratic political system in 1987 and launched an aggressive initiative for domestic liberalization by the early 1990s. During this particular period, a macro or systemic NIC emerged, a reactive initiative for enforcing a sharp structural transformation from a state-led to a market-led regime by dismantling the developmental state and deregulating production and financial relations in an uncontrolled manner that led to the genesis of four micro NICs and the fragmentation of the country's institutional stock.

In fact, a structural transformation of this kind had already been initiated by President Park when the Comprehensive Economic Stabilization Policy of April 1979 was announced to control inflation, actualize market prices, deregulate the financial system, and open up the economy to international competition by lifting the state's control over the domestic and external market competition. This approach was then consolidated with two consecutive IMF standby agreements, signed between July 1983 and March 1987. The policy outcomes of this can be well seen as a nearly one-third deceleration in broad money growth along with a nearly 50 percent decline in inflation, a more than sixfold increase in (real) lending interest rates as well as the transition from a fixed to a multicurrency basket system (Fig. 3.1).

The second part of this period, 1987–1996, stands for an era when unfettered commercial and financial liberalization had gathered systemic momentum in the country's history. In particular, the Kim government (February 1993 to February 1998) executed three financial liberalization reforms in November 1993, December 1994, and July 1995. These reforms were aimed at eliminating state control over finance such as the deregulation of interest rates, abolishment of policy loans, lifting of growth-oriented monetary and credit policy, and liberalization of capital accounts such as lifting bans on foreign borrowing (McKay 2003).

Thus, foreign investors were allowed, inter alia, to invest directly in the South Korean stock markets under ownership ceilings in 1992, and to purchase government and public bonds and equity-linked bonds in 1994. Residents were allowed to invest in overseas securities in 1993, the ceiling on domestic institutional investors' overseas portfolio investment was abolished in 1995, and foreign commercial loans were allowed without government approval (Chang et al. 2001). In addition, banks were authorized to borrow short-term money from international markets, and the *chaebols* could issue bonds and stocks in overseas markets (Chang 2003: 57–63).

Among the consequences of these reforms take place cutting back governmental intervention around a quarter and tightening fiscal policy with a zero budget deficit between 1987 and 1996, further tightening monetary policy and reducing inflation by nearly half on an average, and rampant financialization with a take-off in market capitalization compared to the first part of the period. Despite these steps toward stabilization and deregulation, the country achieved a growth rate, which was only slightly lower than that in the period 1961–1979, a rapid improvement in current account balance, and a steady and strong increase in savings and investment rates from 20 percent and 21 percent, respectively, in the period 1961–1979, to 33 percent in this particular period (Fig. 3.1).

If so, what triggered the crisis of 1997 in South Korea? In terms of G&D governance, underlying the crisis was the fragmentation and drift of financial and industrial governance as a result of a reactive rationality of restructuration as the systemic NIC of the period. This fragmentation created mainly four (micro) NICs. The first was unfettered financial deregulation in public and private sector finance. The second NIC was excessive leverage and overinvestment in production relations, which was complemented or sparked by the first. The third NIC was the rising rent-seeking dialogue between the corporate businesses and the Korean government, underlying the first two NICs through reorganizing the country's institutional stock from a monolithic pro-market and anti-state rationality. The fourth NIC was fragmented industrial governance that ruptured not only the efficient allocation of factors of production but also deranged sectoral development and transitions. These four NICs factored in the crisis of 1997 after unfolding in a drifty process, particularly in the latter part of the period.

The first NIC consisted of two pillars. The first pillar was related to the macro conduct of the country's financial regime. The country's foreign exchange reserves in the Bank of Korea (BOK) had declined to as low as 47 percent of the external short-term debt in 1996 (Wade 1998: 1543). The growth rate of the country's foreign debt rose from 17 percent per annum in the period 1979–1985 to 33 percent per annum between 1994 and 1996. In addition, the external debt of large enterprises increased 64 percent per annum as of GDP between 1994 and 1996, specifically 170 percent increase in 1996. However, the country's foreign debt stock, which stood at 22 percent in 1996, was much lower than the 48 percent limit imposed by the World Bank (WB) as a low-risk threshold. The country's debt-service ratio, 5.8 percent in 1996, was also considerably lower than the WB's warning threshold of 18 percent (Sin and Chang 2003: 39).

Therefore, what exposed the Korean economy to financial shocks in macro financial terms was by and large the large quantity of short-term loans as the lenders refused to roll over their loans, particularly during the upsurge of the South East Asian financial crisis. The nonperforming loans of financial institutions mounted due to a string of large corporate insolvencies and the credit-rating agencies downgraded the country's sovereign rating. This led to the massive outflow of foreign investor funds and depletion of the country's usable foreign exchange reserves. Further, worsening the country's foreign exchange position was the rising expectation of a massive depreciation of the South Korean Won (KRW) (Bank of Korea 2016: 13–14).

The second pillar related to the micro conduct of the financial regime. During the early 1980s, the Korean government imposed an 8 percent limit on the number of bank shares that an individual or *chaebol* could own, and sold government-held shares in commercial banks. Commercial banks were allowed to fix interest rates on regular deposits and loans as well as on corporate bonds (the government de facto held the ability to control credit allocation through various administrative measures). In addition, a liberal licensing policy was adopted for entry into the financial industries without any supervisory measures, resulting in a suboptimal increase in the number of financial firms.

In the period 1985–1997, about 10 new commercial banks and 29 new life insurance companies were established, and the number of merchant banking corporations (short-term finance companies) jumped to 30 percent from 6 percent. The share of these institutions in deposits and loans increased from 25 percent and 36 percent in 1980 to 63 percent and 51 percent in 1992, respectively. In addition, market capitalization grew from 30 percent in 1992 to 41 percent of the country's GDP in 1995, although declining to 23 percent in 1996. Furthermore, the corporate sector's external financing from nonbank financial institutions increased to 21 percent in 1992 from 15 percent in 1980. This increase, expectedly, resulted in a remarkable decline in borrowing from banks to 15 percent in 1992 from 20 in 1980 (Lee et al. 2002: 21–23).

This institutional stock, essentially aimed at transforming the debt-based finance of *chaebols* into equity finance, caused the accumulation of nonperforming loans in the financial sector during the 1990s (Shin and Chang 2005: 428–429). For example, the merchant banks' credit ratio exceeded, in most cases, the limit of 150 percent of their stockholders' equity. These banks were to enjoy higher interest on their loans than on their debts insofar as they could roll over the short-term debt they borrow using interest income from the long-term loans they lend to their clients. As the government left the ratio of short-term debt to the total debt uncontrolled, the ratio of this debt steadily increased from 43 percent in 1992 to 58 percent in 1996. The consequence was the failure of seven merchant banks in servicing their debt in August 1997, and the Bank of Korea had to provide emergency loans at the cost of draining its foreign exchange reserves (Lee 2000: 128–129).

The second NIC had two pillars. First, it became easier for *chaebols* to reach investment credits using cross-loan guarantees among their affiliates, but they slipped into a financial challenge at the end of the period. Second, as a result of easier access to finance, *chaebols* diversified their business areas, and this led to overinvestment in certain key industries.

Gradually the *chaebols* became independent actors in economic governance as a result of their changing relationship with the Korean state and the financial system. During the period when entrepreneurship was controlled by an authoritarian regime, the government was not obligated to organize any political campaign to keep social demands under control.

The democratic system, however, required governments to raise additional funds, mainly from *chaebols*, for their political campaigns (Lee et al. 2002: 20). Consequently, this rent-seeking between the state and the market as the third NIC during this particular period urged the Korean governments to succumb to the deregulated demands of *chaebols*, especially during the 1987 presidential elections to counteract the so-called campaign contributions. This third NIC paved the way for the destruction of a growth-driven credible commitment between the state, banks, and *chaebols*.

Facilitating this rent-seeking coalition was the absence of strong political and social groups that could counterbalance *chaebols'* increasing dominance (Mo and Weingast 2013: 141). In fact, President Chun (1980–1988) and President Roh (1988–1993) had imposed certain measures on the *chaebols* to divest their subsidiaries and to dispose of their speculative real estate holdings, and so on. These attempts, however, faltered to a great extent (the Monopoly Regulation and Fair Trade Act of 1980 effectively curtailed bank loans, cross-shareholding, and debt guarantees of the top 30 *chaebols*).

Under such an institutional setting, *chaebols* first seized the power to extend credit opportunities without any restriction, becoming possible due to two factors. First, beginning with the privatization of banks in 1983, the *chaebols* started purchasing large blocks of stocks in these banks. By 1988, the top 30 *chaebols* owned approximately 30 percent of the total outstanding shares of the banking sector. Their blocks were large enough to influence banks' decisions, albeit limited in percentage. They bought controlling shares of stock in these institutions with the elimination of the limits on ownership of nonbanking financial institutions such as insurance, investment trusts, securities, and merchant banking firms. Subsequently, they earmarked their holdings in these institutions for securing heftier loans through both direct and indirect channels such as mutual debt guarantees that would not be justifiable in official banking terms. Such a relationship enabled the *chaebols*, inter alia, to bypass the regulatory power of the government and therefore to act free from governmental decrees (Haggard and Moon 1990).

The second one was related to the ownership structure in *chaebols*. Ownership control in the top 30 *chaebols* was twofold: the ownership of key member firms by the family and the interlocking of other member firms through circular shareholding. Such an interlocked shareholding aimed at creating necessary capital for investment, which otherwise would have been paid from the conglomerate's own capital. The financial magnitude of these groups was used as strong collateral that banks could rely on. Similarly, *chaebols* could raise more funds from the stock market, thanks to their group affiliation. Further, this affiliation enabled them to spread the risk across their member firms and maintain a higher rate of leverage.

Without this fictitious capital, gross fixed capital formation in the Korean economy could not have increased from 24 percent in 1970 to 34 percent in 1996, with the government share declining from 24 percent to 15 percent in the respective years. This finance-investment circular resulted in the accumulation of domestic financial resources in the hands of the top 30 *chaebols*, accruing 46 percent of total assets, 48 percent of total debts, and 47 percent of total profits in the Korean economy, although employing only 4 percent of the total workforce in 1997 (Shin and Chang 2005: 28–31; Claessens et al. 2000).

As the second pillar of the second NIC, *chaebols* diversified their business areas irrespective of causing duplicative or excess investment in key industries. From 1994 to 1996, facility investment in the manufacturing sector grew by 30 percent in all the industries and by 39 percent in the manufacturing sector. *Chaebols* contributed about 46 percent of this massive investment in heavy industries such as automobiles, petrochemicals, steel, and electronics. Toward this, they used 20 percent foreign currency borrowing (FCB), which was 13 percent in the period 1972–1979 when the average growth rate was much higher. Among the underlying factors were negative growth during 1991–1992 and the receding competitiveness due to rising labor costs (Haggard and Moon 2000). In addition, the Kim Young-sam government (1993–1998) launched the New Economy 100-Day Plan on 22 March 1993 to stimulate the stagnant economic growth, which was far lower than the trend (6 percent), through a massive injection of capital beginning 1993, interest rate cuts, increased supply of facility investment funds, and early implementation of government projects.

Not only did this investment glut trigger a slowdown in return to capital and total factor productivity, but it also caused fragmented industrial governance as the fourth NIC during the period. For example, Samsung's entry into the auto industry in 1994, then an overly saturated market, aimed to make the firm the largest *chaebol* by taking advantage of a technology-intensive sector for upgrading its then light-industry-oriented business structure. The firm, however, did not have necessary infrastructure to achieve this purpose. As of 1993, consumer goods manufacturing constituted only 5 percent of the firm's investment areas (electronic, machinery, and chemical industries constituted 38 percent, service-related industries including finance and information 57 percent). By then competitors Hyundai and Daewoo had heavy-industry-oriented business structures. This infeasible investment increased the Samsung Group's debt ratio from 297 percent in 1993 to 371 percent in 1997 with the launch of the firm's auto business (Shin and Chang 2003: 30–31).

One of the complementary factors for fragmented industrial governance was intragovernment conflict in enforcing economic restructuring under the shadow of rent-seeking between the state and the market. In 1994, a report by the Korea Institute of Economy and Technology, sponsored by the Ministry of Commerce and Industry, drew attention to the risks, inter alia, of the dissipation of economies of scale in the automotive industry and a prospective increase in the overall production costs in the sector fueled by excessive competition in manufacturing facility expansion. The report noted that these risks would result in full elimination of market entry regulation and removal of governmental protection in this sector (Lee 2000: 122). President Kim Young-sam succumbed to Samsung's systematic lobbying initiatives in licensing for gaining entry into the sector under the guise of the then dominant economic logic of spontaneous equilibrium in liberal markets. Besides, President Kim's political roots were in the Pusan region, challenged by the gradual deterioration of major industries owing to rising labor costs, and Samsung proposed to establish its auto manufacturing plant there.

Why did this process of commercial and financial deregulation become the main cause of the 1977 crisis? This process did not aim to phase up the transformation from entrepreneurship during the authoritarian regime into a liberal one through a planned and systemic governance process, underlying the macro NIC in the period. Liberal democratic governance cannot be argued to be worse than an authoritarian one. The argument here is that fragmented liberal democratic governance is worse than a systemic one even if the latter is implemented in an authoritarian manner. The former results in a barely reversible de-linkage between the means and ends of an economic policy, precipitating the genesis and embedding of the above-noted four micro NICs. In this sense, the period, 1980–1996, turned out to be a process when the country's PICs-dominated structure started to turn into a NICs-dominated one. The country's performance was impressive in terms of average growth rates, but the NICs that emerged during this stage underlie the embedding of a fragmented structure in the third period, 1997–2007, of the country's G&D process, thereby turning into the preliminary causes of the institutional trap facing South Korea today.

For this reason, this second period in the country's G&D process from World War II onward is of crucial importance in understanding the current stage of that process. It would thus be useful to further debate the most popular argument about why the crisis of 1997 occurred to clarify our perspective.

Interpreting this view, underlying the crisis was the negative externality of crony capitalism propped by a state-led protective regime (Fischer 1998). In view of the country's impressive economic performance during 1961–1996, per se, it is not tenable to argue that crony capitalism, rent-seeking alliance between the state and private enterprises, was the driving force of G&D during its first period 1961–1979. As Shin and Chang (2003: 48) posit, such an alliance was the case throughout the country's high-growth period. The traditionally corrupt areas were urban planning and defense contracts during the period when the authoritarianism controlled entrepreneurship. But cronyism then extended to manufacturing, as noted above, with the dismantling of strategic industrial policy on performance criteria, financial regulation, and five-year planning as these deregulations eased residual behavior. In other words, cronyism became a micro NIC when the country's G&D process fell into enduring institutional fragmentation, enabling *chaebols* to manipulate system-wide complementarities, in line with their own interests.

Another implication of the argument of crony capitalism is that such a rent-seeking action became possible due to the country's state-led G&D process. It should be noted that the state-led character of the South Korean model did not rest on the enormity of state investment or consumption expenditures. Also, institutional failure did not stem from the declining size of the state's regulatory intervention.

In South Korea, government share in overall investment remained at around 20 percent as of GDP until the beginning of democratization in 1987, and before declined slightly rather than sharply (overall, government investment trended lower, from 21 percent in 1980 to 14 percent in 2014). This rate is well below the average of OECD member countries, 24 percent and 22 percent in the periods 1960–1979 and 1980–2015, respectively. The government's final consumption expenditures remained around 11 percent until the Asian crisis and steadily rose to 15 percent in 2015. The average of the same data for OECD member countries was also 16 percent and 17 percent in the periods 1960–1979 and 1980–2015, respectively.

South Korea, therefore, was not heavily interventionist but an authoritarian entrepreneurial state, implementing a selective and strategic industrial policy particularly in the 1960s and 1970s under a process of controlled liberalization. Its major role was to establish and sustain the coherence of a systemic governance of the South Korean kind, prior to the beginning of institutional fragmentation in the early 1980s.

3.4 Embedding of Institutional Fragmentation, 1997–2007

In the aftermath of the crisis, the IMF program of December 1997 rested on three orthodox measures: (1) macroeconomic consolidation through high interest rates and tight budgetary policy including a small surplus; (2) full deregulation of product and capital markets, abolition of all trade-related subsidies, and upper limit on foreigners' domestic shareholdings; and (3) the establishment of the Financial Supervisory Commission to undertake a supervisory role over financial institutions adopting the Bank for International Settlements' capital adequacy ratio (Bank of Korea 2016: 15).

South Korea's institutional architecture was restructured in line with these measures, even though the country adopted a Keynesian strategy of recovery and initiated a series of welfare programs during the period 2003–2008 under President Roh Moo-hyun. Between the Asian crisis and the housing bubble is an era during which institutional fragmentation in the country's developmental model became embedded with the deepening of market capitalization and external (commercial and financial) liberalization (Pirie 2005; Cheery 2005). External liberalization refers to the sharp cutback in tariff rates, rapid increase in the volume of international trade, and rising foreign direct investment as well as influx of foreign portfolio investment between 1998 and 2005.

The micro NICs that had burgeoned during the earlier period, 1980–1996, became entrenched in this period. First is the embedding of fragmentation in the governments' economic policy between discretionary policy and structural adjustment measures, resulting in a sharp fall in growth rate to 5.5 percent from 7.9 percent in the period 1980–1996 and a sharp increase in unemployment to 4.1 percent from 3.2 percent in the latter period. Second is the embedding of fragmentation in the financial governance of G&D between finance, investment, and entrepreneurial capital with the rampant market capitalization and the increasing share of foreigners in the Korean stock market and banking industry. Third is the embedding of fragmentation in the credible commitment between *chaebols* and the Korean state to developmental targets with the failed attempts to restructure and deregulate the corporate governance regime in the country.

First, economic policy in the period was by and large in parallel with the IMF program in terms of its average impact on key Macroeconomic variables: a tight monetary and fiscal policy, the highest real lending interest rates, and the lowest inflation rates over the last five decades (Fig. 3.1). Officially, the Bank of Korea adopted inflation targeting in April 1998, pursuing an inflation-obsessive monetary policy.

Albeit being in line with the IMF program in broad strokes, economic policy was however not straightforward throughout the period but floating between Keynesian and neoclassical lines. Underlying was an aggressive Keynesian strategy that stimulated quick recovery from negative growth of 5.7 percent in 1998 to 10.7 percent in 1999 and 8.8 percent in 2000. Interest rate in the interbank call market reduced radically to 6.6 percent in July 1998, boosting the economy by increasing liquidity and mitigating financial burden over private enterprises. This rate that has never recorded a one digit figure earlier remained below 5 percent from 1999 and onward. The lending interest rate, usually meeting the short- and medium-term financing needs of the private sector, was lowered to 9.4 and 6.7 percent in 1999 and 2002, respectively, from as high as 15.2 percent in 1998.

In addition to lower inflation levels, the injection of nearly US$ 50 billion public funds to recapitalize financial institutions had also contributed toward liquidity expansion (BOK 2013: 129). During the period, Bank of Korea's monetary policy continued to be accommodative such as reducing the call rate during severe downturns in domestic demand, as was the case between July and August 2001 and August and November 2004. Later, the Bank reversed this accommodative stance due to the improving trend in the real economy from the latter half of 2005 to mid-2006, when it started increasing the call rate (Bank of Korea 2013: 129–140).

Second, in the aftermath of the Asian financial crisis, the country initiated a number of reforms to enhance national financial and commercial infrastructure to global standards by enabling foreigners to invest in the Korean market and making the financial system independent of governmental interventions. For example, with the enactment of the Foreign Investment and Foreign Capital Inducement Act of 1998, the country opened the domestic market to foreign competition including hostile mergers and acquisitions and expanded the range of sectors for foreign investment. As a corollary, in December 1997, the Act on the Establishment of Financial Supervisory Organization was enacted to encourage the new financial regime. The Financial Supervisory Commission and the Financial Supervisory Service were established in April 1998 and January 1999, respectively, to regulate and monitor financial institutions and for revoking licenses of financial institutions as well as for overseeing economic restructuring after the crisis. The executive members of these organizations were predominantly independent of political influence, focusing on financial stability instead of investment and growth.

Rather than increasing investment capital to firms, this transformation capacitated foreign capital to be the market mover in the Korean financial system. Foreign investing in the Korean stock market jumped from 15 percent to 43 percent in 2004 before declining to 30 percent in 2008. Similarly, the share in the Korean banking industry increased from 16 percent in 1997 to 58 percent in 2007 before declining to 50 percent in 2008. Foreign investors, expectedly, aim to maximize their profits within the confines of the newly imposed supervision measures through speculative investment and aggressive funding of consumer loans rather than of long-term corporate lending (patient capital). Such a change transformed the traditional role of the Korean banking sector in intermediating public-private savings and investment and in acting as the agents of state rather than only as profit maximizers (Kim and Yang 2011; Woo 1991: Chaps. 6 and 7).

As a result, these reforms along with those executed in the third period transformed South Korea's bank-based or stakeholder-driven financial structure into a capital market-based financial system. Market capitalization of listed firms increased from an average of 22 percent in the period 1979–1996 to 53 percent in the period 1997–2007.

Third, in corporate governance, owner families, acting as de facto CEO, a function inherited from family members, controlled *chaebols*. In practice, the chairman of a business group had the capacity to appoint members of the board of directors. This ran counter to the minority shareholders' rights as Korean boards convened mainly to approve major decisions by executive officers, regardless of how effectively business operations are conducted. A few outside directors were chosen from those affiliated with controlling families. The chairman could take any decision without seeking consent from the board of directors and is not held responsible for any decision. As seen in the Samsung Group's venture into the automobile industry in 1994, such arbitrary decisions typically resulted in large-scale failures (Hemmert 2012: 93–102; Fan and Wong 2005).

The implications of the IMF program for corporate governance included (1) forcing *chaebols* to reduce their debt-equity ratios to 200 percent from 400 percent in less than two years, (2) prohibiting loan guarantees and internal transactions among *chaebol* affiliate firms, and (3) inducing them to concentrate on core businesses by selling, closing, and swapping peripheral businesses (Shin and Chang 2005: 410). Considering these policy prescriptions, the Korean government first strengthened the roles of outside directors and independent auditors, and attempted to improve transparency and accountability of *chaebols* requiring the 30 largest *chaebols* to attune their financial statements to international standards, as of financial year 1999.

In a bid to incentivize both friendly and hostile mergers and acquisitions, the government raised the limit on foreign equity ownership for Korean firms to 100 percent in late 1998 from 55 percent. In addition, in 1999, firms were required to ensure that outside investors represent at least one-quarter of the board of directors. In practice, however, this regulation changed nothing as the majority of these investors had close relationships with major shareholders. Further, the government did not enforce any regulation such as class action lawsuits and agglomeration of votes for the broader protection of minority shareholders (Chang 2003: 209–212; Kang 2010: 536).

At first glance, the outcome of these reforms is that *chaebols* seemed to have reduced their debt burden. The reality, however, was that they consolidated their finances by selling their assets and increasing cross-shareholding. Under a program entitled the Big Deal Plan, the government initiated to consolidate eight industries and to urge *chaebols* in these industries to focus on their core competencies. This plan, however, also turned out a big failure, apart from the ship engine business. For example, after acquiring LG Semiconductor, Hyundai Electronics incurred huge debts and a plunge in the price of DRAMs. The firm survived because of government pressure on banks to buy its bond issues. To save the combined aerospace business from bankruptcy, the government provided 530 billion Won (KRW). Further, when the three separate unions feared integration and consolidation in the railroad vehicles business, the government had to seek a buyer, and so on (Chang 2003: 189–208).

Further, higher interest rates, 8 percent between 1998 and 2001 as an average, pushed *chaebols* into excessive debt and bankruptcy due to a liquidity crunch, leading to an upsurge in nonperforming loans amounting to 29 percent of Korea's GDP in 2001, particularly during the four years after the crisis. In addition, the private sector's investment expenditures increased at a rate of minus 0.3 percent between 1997 and 2007, and operating profit in the manufacturing sector during this four-year period of restructuring dropped to 6.6 percent from its average of 7.2 in the earlier period.

Exacerbating the country's productive potential was the reality of *distress sale* where Korean companies and financial institutions, mainly those with bright prospects, were sold to foreign firms mainly to overcome those firms' liquidity constraints. The government's perspective that FDI was a driving force for the country to exit from the depressing impact of the crisis pressured domestic institutions to sell their assets to foreigners, in addition to the assurance of various financial incentives and guarantees to the latter such as the government acquiring the nonperforming loans of the firm to be sold, as was the case in the sale of Korea First Bank to Newbridge Capital, a US investment bank, and General Motors takeover of Daewoo Motors (Shin and Chang 2003: 115–116).

The reason why the embedding of fragmentation in economic policy, financial governance, and corporate governance matters is that the country's performance in G&D was managed not on the basis of long-run developmental targets, as was the case during authoritarian entrepreneurship, but on the basis of the government's adoption of an ad hoc policy or the short-term gains of finance and productive capital. This drift of economic policy and finance and corporate governance ended up not only with micro failures such as the bankruptcy of *chaebols* but also the macro ones such as the lowest average growth performance, 5.5 percent as of GDP, from the 1960s onward. Underlying was, inter alia, the decline of annual increase in fixed investment from 10 percent as of GDP during the period 1980–1996 to 2 percent, and the declining rate of increase in total government and household consumption expenditures from 11 percent of GDP in the former to 6 percent in the latter.

3.5   Institutional Trap Between Developmentalism, Deregulation, and Maturation, 2008–2015

The period from 2008 onward witnessed the ebb and flow of the country's G&D process between the resurgence of developmentalism and macroeconomic consolidation, ongoing commercial and financial deregulation, and economic maturation. These three intertwined dynamics factor into the institutional trap of declining growth, rising inequality, and faltering industrial sophistication (the maturation and faltering of industrial sophistication will be elaborated in the subsection examining the country's industrial development).

Broadly, three points exposed the Korean economy to the 2008 crisis. First, the country adopted a capital-intensive growth strategy financed through short-term debt, causing rollover problems and liquidity risk. Second, the volume of stock market capitalization in the Korean economy was on a par with the country's GDP in 2007, and the rate of foreign ownership in the stock market was over 40 percent between 2003 and 2006, although declining to 29 percent in 2008 on the back of large-scale withdrawal of funds by foreign banks. Third, the country's banks had a higher loan-to-deposit ratio, particularly the short-term US dollar liabilities they had borrowed from offshore markets, than any emerging market outside the Baltics, and were, therefore, exposed to substantial credit risk.

In this institutional setting, after the crisis broke out, foreign investors including US hedge funds had rushed for liquidation when taking losses on other investments. Consequently, first, there was outflow of a massive amount of capital, more than 3 percent of the GDP in 2008, and the Won was devalued by around 50 percent between July and November 2008, the sharpest devaluation of any major currency in 2008 and the first half of 2009. In addition, stock values collapsed by approximately 30 percent, and the stock market capitalization rate plummeted to 47 percent of GDP. Second, the country's GDP growth decelerated to 2.8 percent in 2008 with a 4.5 percent decline in the last quarter of 2008. Unemployment rose to 3.6 percent at the end of 2008 from 3.2 percent in 2007. Exports registered an increase of minus 0.3 percent as of GDP in 2008 due to the slowdown in world trade, aggravating the foreign investors' sentiments in the country's then unstable currency market (Pirie 2015; Eichengreen et al. 2012: Chap. 7).

From the fourth quarter of 2008, compelled by deficient domestic demand and shrinking exports, the Korean state responded to the declining domestic business activity by taking an active role in providing investment credit and industrial planning. In particular, the state boosted aggregate demand and improved credit conditions by (1) reducing the policy interest or base rate from 5.25 percent to 2 percent between October 2008 and February 2009; (2) injecting 18.5 trillion Won (KRW), amounting to 1.5 percent of GDP, into the financial system between September 2008 and February 2009; and (3) providing temporary guarantees on rolled-over short-term foreign debts of commercial banks in order to support the banking system and bond markets (Bank of Korea 2013: 146–152; Pirie 2015: 2–5; Shin 2014). It was the ample foreign reserves of the Bank of Korea that had alleviated the potential impact of massive capital outflows on private banks' assets. During that time, foreign reserves were as high as to cover a potential foreign liquidity shock due to the massively accumulated short-term foreign debts. Another factor was the sound financial position of the *chaebols*. The average debt-to-equity ratio of the corporate sector had tumbled to around 100 percent in 2008 from 400 percent in 1997 (Cho 2015: Chap. 15).

In 2009, the government's investment expenditures soared to 21 percent of GDP from 17 percent in 2008, but first retreated to 17 percent in 2010 and continued to steadily decline to 15 percent in 2015 (during this process, the government's final consumption expenditure remained steady at 14 percent to 15 percent of the country's GDP). The share of subsidies and other transfers as of total governmental expense, which had declined from 64 percent in 1996 to 53 percent in 2006, increased to 60 percent on average between 2007 and 2015. Government expenditure on education and R&D, 3.8 percent and 2.4 percent as of GDP during the period 1997–2007, increased to 4.6 and 3.7 percent, respectively, in the period 2008–2015.

As a result, the country's growth and export performance resumed and credit conditions eased, largely due to the countercyclical measures noted above, particularly with the state announcing the largest fiscal stimulus among the OECD members between 2008 and 2010. In fact, the Korean government also avoided huge budget deficits due to the rapid growth recovery in 2009 and thereafter. Rather, the government budget yielded 1 percent surplus between 2008 and 2015, except a deficit of 1.3 in 2009. Furthermore, the consumer price index (CPI) remained below the central bank's target, declining from 4.6 in 2008 to 1.3 percent in 2014.

Albeit the countercyclical measures noted above, the country did not execute systemic reforms in its growth model, but deregulation continued to deepen during the period. First, to a great extent, the regulatory framework of the country's financial system was left intact, and the market capitalization ratio rebounded to its precrisis level, though slackening later. Second, the OECD's economy-wide regulation index for the country, which measures the degree to which policies promote or inhibit competition in the area of product market, continued to decline from 2.56 percent in 1998 to 1.88 in 2013. This indicates the abolition of economic regulations, which continued in 2014 with the launch of the *cost-in cost-out* system to cap the regulatory burden over the firms in line. Third, the taxes on international trade, as of governmental revenue, continued to steadily decline from 10 percent in 1989 to 2 percent in 2015, as of total revenue. The volume of international trade as a percentage of GDP, sum of exports and imports, continued to increase from 77 percent in 2007 to 110 percent in 2011, but declined to 84 percent in 2015. The issue here is not the continued deregulation but the fact that all these deregulations unfolded in a process fragmentation regardless of their overall negative impact in generating lower growth, higher inequality, and slackening industrial sophistication.

Overall, during this period, large foreign reserves consolidated the financial structure of firms, and relatively stable house prices and a sound government budget underpinned the quick recovery of the Korean economy in 2009 and thereafter (Tsutsumi et al. 2010). However, the policy mix adopted in this last period resulted in a 46 percent slowdown in the country's GDP over the period 2008–2015 compared to a 5.1 percent average growth between 1997 and 2007. Specifically, the current account surplus had augmented from 0.3 in 2008 to 7.7 in 2015. Though a positive indicator, such high surplus points to weak domestic demand due, inter alia, to the strong household debt, stagnant service sector productivity, struggling small- and medium-sized enterprises, and extreme dependence on exports. (In particular, household's debt as of disposable income increased from 131 percent in 2002 to 163 percent in 2012, whereas household's net savings of disposable income declined from 10 percent in 2005 to 6 percent in 2012. In addition, household's financial assets increased from 45 percent as of GDP to 59 percent in 2015. In other words, the households' budgets have both become increasingly debt-dependent and financialized, thereby reducing private consumption and increasing their vulnerability.)

In brief, the debt stock of the total economy increased from 580 percent as of GDP in 2008 to 669 percent as of GDP in 2015, even though this rate is much lower than the OECD average of 851 percent and 933 percent as of GDP during the same years, respectively. The country's short-term foreign debt declined from 52 percent of its total debt in September 2008 to 27 percent in December 2015. Foreign exchange reserves rose to US\$ 368 billion in December 2015 from US\$ 201 billion at the end of 2008, 3.4 times higher than short-term foreign debt. Consequent is the increasing vulnerability of the households due to increasing financialization and indebtedness of their balances. Private sector indebtedness is 163 percent as of GDP, a relatively higher rate than the OECD average of 148 percent in the period 2008–2015.

3.6   Floating Industrial Sophistication

In terms of industrial governance, the country's declining G&D performance over the past six decades arises out of the fragmentation of sectoral development, R&D efforts, and educational strategies. Underlying is the basic NIC in the area of industrial governance. From the 1980s onward, in particular the early 1990s, the Korean state transformed into a network state and confined its role in industrial development to the ad hoc coordination of relations of production and financial and tax incentives, thereby leaving the active governance of production to the private sector (Larson and Park 2014: 348). As a result, the state continued to steer industrial development, but this time without a systemic governance strategy in which it takes a leading role in the organized determination and execution of G&D strategies at the level of production, finance, and wealth distribution.

The micro consequence of this has already been documented in the previous section with reference to the fragmentation of financial and corporate governance over the last four decades. Over this timespan, the main intercourse between macro industrial development and microfinancial and corporate governance has emerged in the weakening of credible commitment between corporate strategies and the country's developmental targets, culminating in increasing information asymmetry and transition costs in the sectoral distribution of private investment (Hundt 2009). At this stage, the following is an account of macro dynamics of that fragmentation at the level of the country's industrial policy.

The country's industrial policy in the 1980s and the early 1990s focused on industrial rationalization for unpromising industries and insolvent enterprises. The 1980 stabilization program, for example, aimed to reduce excessive capacity in sectors such as power generators, automobiles, construction, and heavy electric machinery by merging unpromising or insolvent enterprises in these sectors. The strategic focus of the industrial policy changed from selected and directed intervention to one of industry neutral and functional in the 1980s. The Industry Promotion Act of 1986 was, for example, enacted to unify the promotion acts for seven specific industries such as machinery, electronics, and textiles, extending the scope of industrial promotion to all manufacturing industries. The Industrial Development Act of 1999 was enacted to eliminate the negative externalities of the Asian crisis on the country's industrial sector, further extending the scope of industrial promotion to the non-manufacturing industries.

The hallmark of this strategy has been to support small- and medium-sized enterprises (SMEs) to unleash a balanced growth strategy by eradicating structural imbalances embedded by the selective industrial policy. The Korean state's industrial support has thus been in the form of strengthening the SMEs' competitiveness base, consolidating their cooperative relations with large firms, stimulating their technological development, and supporting exports and overseas expansion during this period. Consequent was the increase of the SMEs' contribution to the total value added from 35 percent in 1980 to 42 percent of total value added in 2000 (Koo 2013; Bae 2001; Cheery 2005). As a corollary, beginning with the 1990s, in particular in the aftermath of the Asian financial crisis, the Korean state focused on promoting technology- and knowledge-intensive industries. In 1997, the Special Act on Venture Firm Promotion aimed to support newly established venture SMEs, particularly in ICT-related sectors that had a major role in achieving this purpose through incentives such as the reduction of foundation capital, permission of plants in universities and institutes, and the provision of information-related management.

In the period 1997–2008, the key focus of the industrial policy was promoting regional strategic industries and creating innovative clusters. The export-oriented industrial policy and heavy and chemical industrial policy during the 1960s and the 1970s widened the spatial disparity as a result of the bipolar concentration of industries in the Capital and in the South East region. In addition, these complexes lost their competitiveness due to lack of R&D capabilities, insufficient knowledge-based services, difficulty in attracting high-quality workers, and so on. Arising out of the antipathy toward the loopholes of the pre-1980 era, industrial clusters aimed to bring private and local initiatives together in order to boost national competitiveness and promote urban and regional growth, particularly after the Asian crisis.

The Participatory Government program of 2002 had focused on achieving balanced national development by promoting regional innovation and cluster policies (Uttam 2012). Four policy objectives underlie the regional innovation policies: (1) providing the basis for the establishment of regional innovation systems through the organization of regional innovation councils consisting of representatives of universities, industries, and research institutions, (2) promoting scientific research and conventions, strengthening universities' innovation capacity in provinces with financial and coordination support, (3) promoting science and technology in the provincial regions by increasing their share in the government's total R&D budget, and (4) establishing industry-university-research center networks. After coming to power in 2008, the Lee Myung-bak government assumed a more extensive coordinational role by developing the regional economic area (REA) for establishing hub-and-spoke type regional clusters with 25 hub complexes and 168 connected complexes. This strategy of expansion was phased out in stages from the individual hub complexes to the neighboring connected complexes to the pan regional cluster by the regional economic areas and to the inter-regional economic area nationwide (Park and Koo 2013).

These efforts in stimulating balanced growth and establishing creative networks produced two effects in the absence of a credible commitment. The first is the drift of sectoral development in the country arising out of the fragmentation of industrial governance. The key indicator of this is the shift away from rapidly growing manufacturing toward slower-growing services with economic maturation. In these sectors, the rapid rise in high-tech manufacturing has not been matched by a similar growth in employment. Workers expelled from the rapidly growing manufacturing sector that accounted for full three-quarters of the *within effect* in 1997–2007 were unable to move into the rapidly growing high-end services such as finance, insurance, and business services due to skill mismatch (*within effect* is the contribution of an individual sector's labor productivity growth to economy-wide productivity growth). These workers ended up self-employed or in small businesses, which had less to do with strong productivity growth and high personal income (Eichengreen et al. 2012, Chap. 3).

Second, despite partly failing in achieving inter-sectoral transition, the country succeeded in increasing the technological intensity of its manufactures and exports. However, this performance declined and remained sluggish from the mid-2000s onward.

In the 1960s and the 1970s, the Korean industrial sector started pursuing technology transfer strategies such as reverse engineering, original equipment manufacturing, and foreign licensing. In the 1980s, South Korea focused on developing indigenous R&D because foreign companies desisted from transferring technologies in the face of firms increasing competitive power in the international markets. The National R&D Program was initiated in 1982 to achieve this purpose, and the ratio of technology imports to business R&D declined from 40 percent in 1981 to 10 percent in the early 1990s, although increasing to 20 percent in the 2000s.

From the 1980s onward, South Korea achieved remarkable performance in increasing the share of high-tech products in its industrial production largely attributable, inter alia, to well-trained human resources in science and engineering and enterprises venturing into high-risk areas. With this, in the 1980s, Korean industries were ranked among the leading countries in memory chips, cellular phones, LCDs, and other technologies in addition to gaining competitive edge in sectors such as shipbuilding, automobiles, home appliances, and telecommunications (Chung and Shu 2007; Kim 1993).

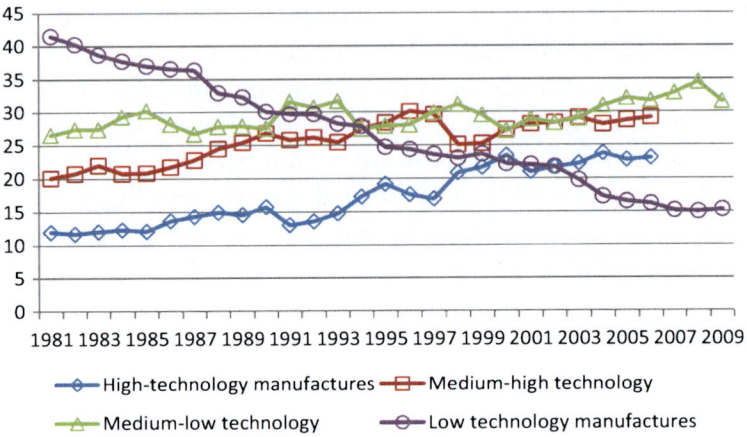

Fig. 3.2 Sectoral value added by technological intensity, 1970–2009. Source: OECD STAN database for structural analysis (2016)

As Fig. 3.2 illustrates, from the early 1980s onward, the total share of high-tech manufactures in semiconductors and communication equipment increased from 12 percent to 23 percent in 2006. Medium-high-tech manufactures—such as automobiles, iron and steel products, and petrochemical products—increased from 20 percent in 1980 to 29 percent in 2006. The medium-low-tech manufacturing such as ships and plastic products increased from 25 percent in the early 1970s to 30 percent in the mid-2000s. Low-tech manufactures such as textiles plummeted rapidly from 60 percent in 1970 to 15 percent in 2009 (OECD 2017). The country's high-tech manufacturing exports steadily increased from 15 percent in the late 1980s to 32 percent in the first half of 2000s, but declined later and remained stagnant at around 27 percent until the mid-2010s (World Bank 2017).

The other causes of a slowdown in economic growth, in addition to the two noted above, in terms of the country's industrial governance, are coordinational failures in R&D and educational strategies. First, in the 1980s and the 1990s, each ministry founded its own R&D program based on a loose long-term plan, causing coordinational problems such as duplication of research efforts, delineation of R&D areas among different ministries, interministerial R&D priority setting, and the efficient allocation of the R&D budget. In order to overcome these challenges, the Minister of Science and Technology was promoted to the rank of deputy minister, becoming a vice-chairman of the National Science and Technology Council. The Ministry was responsible for the coordination of the government research institutes and to guide all research activities in the public sector (Yim 2005). In 2008, this organization was completely revised in order to strengthen the capacity of the National Science and Technology Council (NSTC). With its continuing direct affiliation with the president, the NSTC began to coordinate the formulation and implementation of science, technology, and innovation strategy in association with the newly founded Ministry of Education, Science and Technology and the Ministry of Knowledge Economy.

In contrast, from the 1990s onward, the country focused on creative research and future-oriented research (Chung and Shu 2007). In the face of the Asian crisis, the country's R&D expenditures remained stagnant at around 2.4 percent as of GDP in the period 1997–2006, but gathered significant momentum in the IT sector reaching 3.4 percent on average in the period 2007–2013. The private sector's total share increased from 36 percent in 1980 to 75 percent in the 2000s. However, it is argued that the country's high R&D expenditures are yet to generate higher outputs in terms of patents, scientific results, and new products (Schüller et al. 2012: 109).

The country's patent performance increased from only 1000 in 1980 to 164,000 in 2014 with a 17 percent steady increase per annum on average. South Korea thus gained world prominence in areas such as ICTs, pharmaceuticals, advanced materials, and automotive. However, the country's universities produce very few high-impact publications by OECD standards primarily because the research system has always concentrated on applied and development-oriented research, supplying technology for industrial R&D (OECD 2016: 2).

In parallel with increased R&D expenditures, the Korean civil society continued to leave a considerable amount of their disposable income for educational expenses, 30 percent in 2008, even though the returns on education are low by OECD standards in terms of employment rates and salaries. The gross enrollment rate increased from 7 percent in the early 1970s to nearly 100 percent in the 2010s. The country's performance in

PISA indicators steadily averaged around 520–550 in science, mathematics, and reading in the period 2000–2015. In mathematics and reading, the country outperformed all OECD countries on an average during the period 2000–2015, lagging Finland and Japan in science.

Contrary to this impressive performance in scientific education, the total share of vocational training schemes declined to 24 percent in 2010 from 42 percent in 1995 due to the fact that vocational training is regarded as an education for underperformers and for a low-wage job in a setting where a generalist tertiary education has been available nearly for everyone. As a result, a huge skills gap is formed. The share of inactive population among those with tertiary education was around 22 percent in 2009 and 20 percent in 2015, the highest among the OECD countries (OECD 2016: 49). On-the-job training is also quite low, only 12.8 percent in 2005, far lower than the OECD average of 37.1 percent (Witt 2014: 225–227). Very often, Korean employers complain about this gap arguing that the time required for training young people to start a job after graduating is as long as 20 months (OECD 2010: 109).

3.7   Fragmentation Versus Democratization

The political structure in the country has been stable over the last three decades regarding the regular succession of presidents in four to five years from 1987 onward, as illustrated in Table 3.1. Political competition from democratization onward, albeit extreme volatility in the development of political parties, has been by and large among the predecessors of the two major political parties, the conservative democratic Grand National Party (GNP) and the Progressive Democratic Party (DP). The New Millennium Democratic Party of 1998–2003 was left-wing/progressive, merging with the other two to form the current Democratic Party. The New Korea Party of 1993–1998 was conservative, merging with another party to form the GNP. The conservative and progressive are defined in Korean terms with reference to security and foreign policy alignment. The GNP of Korea defends free-market economy and close relations with the United States with a more principled approach to North Korea. The DP, however, defends reconciliation with North Korea and a pragmatist

Table 3.1 The presidents and incumbent parties in the South Korean politics, 1948–2016

Elections	1948 91% 1952 74% 1956 70% 1960 97%	1960 82%	Interregnum	1963 46% 1967 51% 1971 53% 1972 99% 1978 99%	1979 97%	1980 99% 1988 90%
Incumbency	July 1948–1960	Apr. 1960–1962	Mar. 1962–1963	Dec. 1963–1979	Dec. 1979–1980	Sep. 1980–1988
President	Syngman Rhee	Yon Bo-seon	Park Chung-hee	Park Chung-hee	Choi Kyu-hah	Chun Doo-hwan
Party	NARKKI—LP	DP—NDP	Military	DRP	Independent	DJP

Elections	1987 36%	1993 42%	1997 40%	2002 49%	2007 49%	2012 52%
Incumbency	Feb. 1988–1993	Feb. 1993–1998	Feb. 1998–2003	Feb. 2003–2008	Feb. 2008–2013	Feb. 2013–2016
President	Roh Tae-woo	Kim Young-sam	Kim Dae-jung	Roh Moo-hyun	Lee Myung-bak	Park Geun-hye
Party	DJP	DLP—NKP	NCNP-NMDP	NMDP-OUP	GNP-SP	SP

DJP Democratic Justice Party, *DP* Democratic Party, *DRP* Democratic Republican Party, *GNP* Grand National Party, *NCNP* National Congress for New Politics, *NDP* New Democratic Party, *NKP* New Korea Party, *NMDP* New Millennium Democratic Party, *LP* Liberal Party, *SP* Saenuri Party diplomacy with the United States (Park 2012; Delury and Kaple 2006: 744–754).

Despite their diverse approaches, the country's governments have converged in forming and sustaining an idiosyncratic neoliberal model consisting of macroeconomic austerity and ad hoc countercyclical measures, commercial-financial deregulation, a passive industrial policy, and increasing inequality of income in the face of the coverage of the social safety net. There were mainly three ad hoc countercyclical actions throughout this process: slight expansion of money supply and twofold increase in government investment expenditures in 1997–1998; two and a half times increase in government consumption expenditure during the Roh Moo-hyun government; and a tenfold increase in government expenditures in 2008–2009. However, these actions did not generate any path-diverging impact (President Roh Moo-hyun of 2003–2008 is believed to have embarked on establishing a truly welfare state. During his presidency, however, the Gini coefficient increased from 0.28 in 2003 to 0.31 in 2007, and real wages grew only around half of labor productivity, even though public social expenditures increased more than 40 percent).

Examined in terms of the policy strategies adopted by successive incumbent governments, it turns out that despite the two above-noted facts they did not formulate or implement their policy strategies under the optimizing influence of long-term developmental goals. Instead, they governed in the grip of sluggish political democratization, unbridled economic deregulation, and faltering social policies. As a result, with democratization, the country's presidential political regime, in the absence of active and systemic developmental governance, failed in governing the complications of economic efficiency, social equity, and political democratization in a manner that strikes a trade-off between time rushes and time lags, although per capita income and industrial maturation increased.

There are, inter alia, three NICs in the area of political governance that underlie the above-noted institutional drift and fragmentation in the country's economic G&D. The first is the country's presidential system, which is drawn on appointed bureaucrats rather than elected politicians. The second is the weakening coherence between governments and bureaucrats in making public policy, and the third is the weakening intra-government coherence in executing economic reforms.

Over the last 60 years, South Korea had a presidential executive system with changing institutional structures. The major components of this system are (1) the president, directly elected by the public from 1987 onward, (2) the prime minister, appointed by the president, and (3) the executive systems including the office of the president directly affiliated with the president, and the ministries affiliated with the prime minister. The prime minister assists the president and implements his orders, and the ministries report directly to the president rather than the prime minister. It is the office of the president, founded in 1998, that coordinates policy dialogue between the president and the ministries through the agency of presidential secretariats.

The senior secretary to the president for economic affairs, for instance, acts as a de facto coordinator of six ministries: Ministry of Strategy and Finance; Ministry of Food, Agriculture, Forestry and Fisheries; Ministry of Knowledge Economy; Ministry of Land, Transport and Maritime Affairs; Fair Trade Commission; and the Financial Services Commission. Central agencies such as the Economic Planning Board also play a similar role over the ministries. The dominance of presidential secretariats and central agencies in the face of a minor role of the prime minister at the level of policy formulation and implementation has been criticized for being anti-democratic as more than 80 percent of the former's staff has not been democratically elected (Jung 2015).

A similar anti-democratic structure manifests itself in the dialogue between the presidents and their parties. Korean politics is a partyless system where parties have neither an extensive and elaborate organization nor a formal rank-and-file membership across the country, but compete with each other through programmatic linkages. The structure of political parties has been extremely volatile with frequent closure, mergers, and registrations. For example, nearly 16 political parties disappeared in 2008, while 8 new political parties registered, and 3 merged with others or changed their names. Such a floating existence prevents parties from acting as independent entities, exposing them to the manipulations of presidents and bureaucrats for their self-serving interests. In other words, political parties turn into a means for the president to manifest himself though instrumentalizing their programs and campaigns (Hellman 2014).

A president-guided power competition in a fragmented political landscape where political parties have lost their intermediary role between state and society encourages presidents to abstain from regulating market action in the face of the enduring rent-seeking coalition between the Korean governments and the *chaebols* (Kang 2002). The coordinative role of secretariats is not something necessarily bad, but they function within the confines of this flawed trade-off and keep bottom-up democratic demands for equity away from deranging this coalition, causing a deficit of socioeconomic democracy.

Second, the coherence of the Korean *state governance* on the basis of the credible commitment between the government and bureaucrats has weakened due to changes in its institutional underpinnings and the change of administrational cadres with each successive government. The adoption of the new public management (NPM) concept after the Asian crisis as a requirement of IMF's structural adjustment shattered 'the conventional administrative culture and institutions of integrity, cohesion, continuity, stability, and predictability based on hierarchical authority with the executive branch'. The frequent change of administrational cadre further complicated this fragmentation due to sharpening the short-termism of economic governance in the model. In addition, the establishment of many parallel organizations, in particular committees and social policy apparatuses to counter maneuver the critiques of anti-democracy over the presidential structure and to meet increasing public service demand, respectively, has further exacerbated the coherence in state governance (Jung 2014: 25–26). Thus, the bureaucracy has become deformed, and the means by which it could achieve its end—state power to regulate—have become marginalized. The only remaining option is drifting under the conflicting policy priorities of successive governments.

As an explicit indicator of this fact, the third is that there emerged a conflict between various ministries on how to formulate and implement policy changes. For example, in the mid-1990s, officials in the Ministry of Finance and Economy (MFE) were pro-reform, whereas the Ministry of Trade and Industry (MTI) adopted a more conservative attitude toward liberal deregulations. The former's view was also supported by the hardcore liberal economists of the Korea Institute for International Economic Policy, a think tank funded by the MFE. The MTI was directly in charge of trade negotiation and domestic industries, drawing attention to the risks of reckless diversification of *chaebols'* business areas after the elimination of entry barriers. Perhaps due to this practical experience, the MTI defended a more gradual and prudent strategy maintaining the means for state to intervene and protect the market until Korean businesses could consolidate their financial structure and international competitiveness, and build a market governance regime that would enable businesses to minimize the costly outcomes of information asymmetries such as excessive investment in a sector (Lee 2000: 126).

Overall, it is obvious that political democracy in South Korea has relatively consolidated in terms of turnover of power between ideologically opposite parties, successful inclusion of leftists and progressives in the political regime, overcoming social strife and politico-economic shocks such as the Asian crisis and the impeachment of President Roh Moo-hyun in 2004 within the boundaries of the democratic regime, and so on (Chaibong 2008). Equally obvious, though, is that the Korean political regime assigns systemic power to presidents; restrains elected politicians or political parties from becoming influential in state governance; and fails in institutionalizing robust political party structures, in eliminating the divisive impact of region-based political competition, and in coordinating the bureaucracy and private economic actors in building up a new mode of developmental governance.

Underlying this is that the three NICs restrain the country's political and economic actors from formulating long-term developmental goals, from implementing intercomplementary short-term policy strategies in line with the long-term goals, and from enabling civic actors to actively participate in politics to demand appropriate welfare and working conditions.

3.8   Inequality as a Complement of Nonsynchronous Development

From the early 1980s onward, the country's socioeconomic structure passed through erratic development between inegalitarian and egalitarian lines under the aegis of neoliberal restructuring and political populism, precipitating de-linkage between the socioeconomic pillars of G&D and its industrial basis. For example, the contribution of consumption expenditures to GDP was around 80 percent on average during the period of authoritarian entrepreneurship. Later, this rate declined approximately to 50 percent and is presently stable at that level. Substituting domestic consumer demand is the steady growth in net exports from 14 percent to 51 percent during the periods 1961–1979 and 2008–2014, respectively. First, such a disparity exposes the country to the risk of high export dependency in the face of rising competition from China; second, it accelerates debts and decreases household savings. Foremost, the so-called de-linkage wreaks havoc on the productive and innovative capacity of the country by preventing the institution of a truly democratic mode of economic, corporate, and industrial governance to rebuild system-wide complementarities. In the following paragraphs, the so-called fragmentation has been examined with reference to social policy and industrial relations (IRs).

Korea's social policy can be entitled as a *productivist coalition* in the 1960s and 1970s when public assistance for the poor remained minimal. The coalition aimed at rewarding wage earners with palliative benefits as a complementary tool for a process of rapid economic progress and political legitimacy.

The Health Insurance Act of 1963 confined benefits only to workers employed in firms with 300 plus workers on a noncompulsory basis, which was shortly abandoned in the absence of any sanction. The second national Health Insurance Act of 1976 made it compulsory for all large firms employing more than 500 workers to enroll in the scheme. This health insurance was implemented at 486 firms at the outset. By the late 1970s, the new medical insurance program covered only 20 percent of the employed population, although it was extended to workers in smaller firms in the late 1970s and the early 1980s. In this regard, the striking feature of this period, 1961–1987, was sluggish development of social welfare rights despite quadrupling growth rates (Yang 2013: 464–466).

In the late 1980s and the early 1990s, the Korean social policy evolved into a *progressive coalition* as a policy strategy to expand the scope of social policy in order to protect the weak and redistribute wealth and resources across households by including previously excluded self-employed workers and dependents into the existing social insurance model. The National Pension Act was enacted in 1986 with the National Pension Plan (NPP) to take effect in 1988. On the basis of the social insurance model, the NPP's scope was extended to small firms employing five plus employees and to self-employed workers in 1997. The coverage of healthcare reform and medical insurance was also extended to self-employed workers in 1988 and 1989, respectively (Peng and Wong 2008: 74–77).

From the latter half of the 1990s, Korea's social policy turned into a *new productivist coalition* aimed at increasing industrial competitiveness by lowering labor costs and mitigating social risks by extending the coverage of social welfare programs (Peng and Wong 2008: 65). In this context, social expenditures in the country steadily increased from 2.7 percent in 1990 to 10.4 percent in 2014. In the period 1998–2003, President Kim Dae-jung extended four social insurance schemes to cover the whole country or to all employees (The National Pension Scheme, National Health Insurance, Industrial Accident Compensation Insurance, and Employment Insurance). The Kim government, in addition, introduced the National Basic Livelihood Security System in 1999 to modernize public assistance so as to cover all citizens including those between the ages of 18 and 60. President Roh Moo-hyun (2003–2008) extended the scope of childcare services, community welfare programs for the elderly and disabled, and active labor market policies for the unemployed, in addition to introducing Long-Term Care Insurance, the fifth social insurance care program for the elderly.

Despite the rapid change in coverage from individual workers to households, the country's social welfare programs still fall short of covering a large number of nonregular workers. The main social insurance programs, excluding industrial accidents insurance, cover only 30 percent to 33 percent of nonregular workers. The total share of nonregular workers increased from 44 percent in the period 1989–1997 to 50 percent in the period 1998–2007, although declining to 33 percent in the period 2008–2015. Furthermore, the same programs also have income-based discrimination. The coverage ratio of national pension is only 26 percent for poor households while 58 percent for nonpoor ones. Poor households here refer to those with income below the national minimum cost of living (Kim 2010b: 161–162).

As a result, social welfare programs in the country have become more universal, on the one hand, and have deepened income inequality and stratification between regular and nonregular workers and between high- and low-income groups, on the other. The Gini coefficient declined first from 0.39 in 1980 to 0.24 in 1992, but rose steadily to 0.31 in 2007 and remained stagnant by and large around 0.30 until 2016. The ratio of income from the highest-income groups to the lowest-income groups increased from 3.2 percent in 1993 to 8.4 in 2015, even though GDP per capita grew 5.6 percent compared to the OECD average of 1.7 percent.

The evolution of Korean industrial relations (IRs) can also be categorized broadly into three periods: authoritarianism from the early 1960s to democratization, democratization during the late 1980s, and dissolution from the mid-1990s onward.

In the first period, the Korean state had adopted an equality of income strategy on the basis of asset transfers under a shared growth perspective and employment creation through public work schemes and infrastructure investments. An effective no-layoff policy and high real wage increases at large firms, inter alia, served as the enterprise-level complementarity of this strategy (the average increase in real wages was 11.3 percent between 1968 and 1979). However, the state banned industrial unions and allowed only enterprise unions to preclude political action to come out of organized labor (Fleckenstein and Lee 2017: 168).

In the second period, political democratization in 1987 provided workers with the right to organize and to bargain collectively, paving the way for the formation of strong, independent, and democratic unions in key industries like the automobile sector. Trade union density increased sharply from 13.8 percent in 1987 to 18 percent in 1989, but declined to 10 percent in 2012. The growth of real wages in the period 1987–1992 was 10.1 percent while labor productivity increased around 6 percent, as illustrated at Fig. 3.3.

However, in the third period, 1993–2015, the Korean state pursued a suppressive strategy over trade unions in order to curb the labor costs of *chaebols* through systematic industrial regulations such as the permission of layoffs in case of managerial needs and banning firms to pay wages to full-time union officials in 2010 (see Fig. 3.3). During this period, real wage increase plummeted to 3.7 percent on average, albeit two times

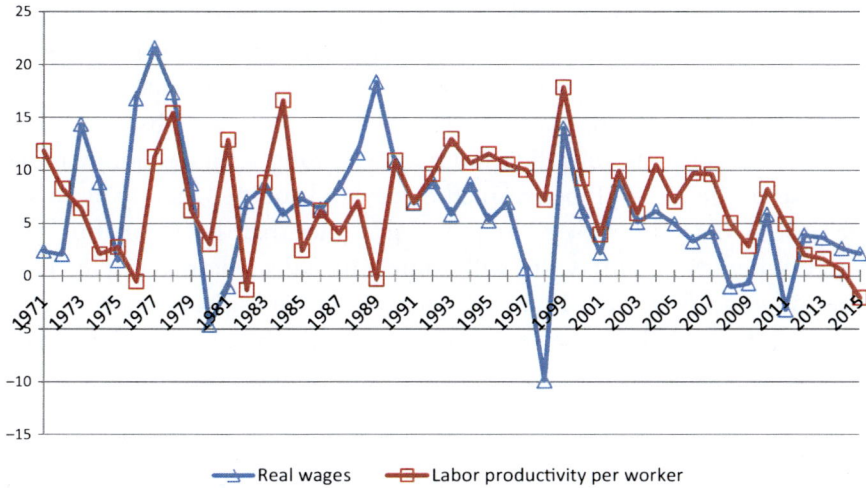

Fig. 3.3 Labor productivity and real wages in South Korea, 1971–2015. Source: Korea Labor Institute (2017)

higher rate of labor productivity. Another indicator is that labor disputes plummeted from 1071 in the period 1985–1992 to 165 in the period 1992–2014.

Instead of collective conflict, in the third period, industrial relations revolved around the strategic choices of enterprises for higher competitiveness with the adoption of Japanese-style new managerial strategies on the basis of higher wages to skilled workers in return for loyalty and higher productivity. This action ended with no-strike declarations in many *chaebols* including LG, Samsung, POSCO, and Hyundai Heavy Industries (Yang 2013: 469). However, it is well documented that there is no standard transformation toward the shareholder model, but a path-dependent change between adversarial relationship under an authoritarian labor-exclusivist governance (Hyundai), management domination with high remuneration under a union-free governance structure (Samsung), a collaborative model in the presence of a militant trade union through an inclusive system of governance and performance-contingent employability (LG), and so on (Kong 2013).

The mixed blessings of the country's socioeconomic performance are deeply rooted in the political mediation of industrial and socioeconomic governance. In this regard, the socioeconomic performance of political parties, particularly from 1987 onward, matters only for alleviating the social pressure arising out of wage constraints and rising income inequality. Throughout this period, public policy in the country was obsessed solely with macroeconomic consolidation than with long-term development on the basis of the trade-off between efficiency and equity. Underlying this is the bureaucracy rather than the political parties that determine how the policy schemes of presidents will come into effect. For example, Kim Dae-jung and Roh Moo-hyun articulated welfare improvement as their core national agenda. However, bureaucrats in the economic units revised the welfare plans, Productive Welfare Initiative and Social Vision 2030, respectively, in line with the neoliberal economic restructuration.

Such actions marginalize the role of political parties in mediating the socioeconomic demands of low-income groups, thereby neutralizing civic organizations lobbying for social justice at the level of party politics (civic movement groups in the country are influential not only in articulating the interests of low-income groups but also in designing social policies, as was done during the passage of the National Basic Livelihood Security Act of 1999). In this regard, trade unions have been deprived of their right to actively engage in political activism under the shadow of the country's authoritarian past, and there has been a face-saving social dialogue mechanism.

Social pacts turn out to be main corporatist platforms where major IRs and social policy arrangements were made, ranging from basic labor rights and job creation to social policy reforms and working time arrangements. Further, more than 90 percent were implemented. For example, in 1998, a social pact was concluded between the Korean Confederation of Trade Unions (KCTU), the Federation of Korean Trade Unions (FKTU), and the Federation of Korean Industries (FKI). The pact was structured on a trade-off between the acceptance of layoff in cases of managerial need and the compensation of arising social risks through social safety nets (Lee and Lee 2003: 511–513).

The rationale underlying social pacts was to reduce labor costs in an export-dependent country in order to enable *chaebols* to maintain their international competitiveness and compensate risks through social safety net programs. The Korean Tripartite Commission (KCT) was officially formed in 1999 to achieve this major purpose through a process of coordination between the state, business, and labor. Members of KCT included national employers' associations (KEF), KCTU, and FKTU as well as representatives of political parties. The Commission was then renamed as the Economic and Social Development Commission in 2007 under a new vision to extend the scope of organized conciliation from enterprise to industry level by establishing industry-level tripartite councils and regional tripartite councils. However, 'it has not been able to function satisfactorily, due to repeated withdrawals, or restricted participation, of both employer and trade union representatives', as noted by the OECD (2000: 49). Among the other pacts, the Social Pact to Overcome the Global Economic Crisis was formed in 2009 on a tripartite basis to secure employment in return for wage restriction, avoiding mass unemployment and maintaining international competitiveness (Yang 2010).

Overall, the nonsynchronous economic and political development has caused a fragmentation and drift in the entitlement of social rights. The productivity coalition, progressive coalition, and the new productivity coalition represent the synchronous trends of universalization of social rights and growing income inequality. Similarly, the trends of authoritarianism, democratization, and re-authoritarianism in IRs have, respectively, generated equal upswings in real wages and labor productivity, much higher wages than productivity, and much lower wages than productivity. A part of this fragmentation is that either the state or a state-business alliance sets the stage for the evolution of socioeconomic dynamics of G&D in the country. In the absence of a genuine democratic culture, organized labor and civic organizations were unable to engage political exchange with the incumbent governments, causing a democratic deficit. The Korean state attempted to fill this gap through face-saving social pacts to ensure political legitimacy.

3.9   Conclusion

South Korea achieved high growth and rapid industrial sophistication with relative improvement in income inequality during the first period of its G&D process, 1961–1979. The country sustained high growth, industrial sophistication, and further improved equality of income during the second period, 1980–1996. However, the decline in average growth rate was quite sharp along with a rapid increase in income inequality, although industrial sophistication continued in the third period, 1997–2007. In the last period, 2008–2015, the sharp decline in growth continued with no change in income inequality, and industrial sophistication decreased swiftly.

The country's first period was neatly summarized in Chap. 1. The second period represents the genesis of institutional fragmentation and drift. Why did the country adopt a strategy of rampant liberal deregulation? The explanation is that to react to a state-led developmental model in the first period considering that the crisis had ended. Despite the high growth and declining inequality through this period, the negative impact of time rush in institutional restructuring manifested itself in the crisis of 1997, arising out of the fragmentation and drift of financial and corporate governance.

The country's rush to financial and commercial liberalization resulted first in the mushrooming of financial intermediaries such as commercial banks, life insurance companies, merchant banking corporations, precipitating excessive credit expansion to a degree far beyond the leverage limits of these intermediaries and in rampant market capitalization. The unregulated structure of corporate and financial governance enabled *chaebols* to have an excessively high leverage ratio and accumulate short-term external debt in foreign currency to make undue and duplicative investment in nonproductive sectors, causing the finance sector to incur huge nonperforming loans. A contributing factor was the expansionary fiscal and monetary policy pursued by Kim Young-sam (1993–1998) during this stage of overinvestment, which is an explicit indicator of rising information asymmetry in industrial governance. Thus, the mechanisms of political, industrial, and financial governance unfolded in a process of drift and finally evolved into the crisis of 1997.

The third period features the embedding of fragmentation in economic policy, financial governance, and corporate governance. The country's economic policy ebbed and flowed between countercyclical and procyclical policy strategies including inflation targeting. The country passed through a rapid process of external, financial, and commercial deregulation such as friendly or hostile mergers and acquisition and expansion of a range of sectors eligible for foreign investment. Corporate governance became further deregulated along with rampant market capitalization, causing the shareholder model to become embedded in the area of corporate finance. However, corporate governance reform failed to drive *chaebols* to focus on their core competences in improving transparency and accountability, culminating in declining profitability, rising indebtedness and bankruptcy of those in high debt due to rising interest rates. During this period, output and employment were the lowest from the 1960s and 1980s onward, respectively. Another negative consequence was that foreigners were the market movers in finance and banking.

The third period ended with the devaluation of the Won by more than 50 percent, the sharpest of its kind in 2008 and 2009, due to the outflow of a massive amount of foreign capital and stock values collapsed by 30 percent along with the sharp drop in output, employment, and exports. However, the tolerable levels of government debt and sound financial position of *chaebols* as well as Bank of Korea's foreign reserves enabled the country to initiate action for overcoming the institutional trap unfolding at the beginning of the fourth period (2008–2015) by applying massive countercyclical measures. These measures were much stronger and more extensive than those applied during and after the Asian crisis, including the largest fiscal stimulus among the OECD countries and more than 60 percent decline in lending interest rates.

However, the key sources of fragmentation and drift in the previous periods remained intact to a great extent. The economic administration was aimed at ensuring macroeconomic consolidation rather than at making structural changes to erect a complementary system on the basis of workable mutuality between efficiency, equity, and technological advancement. Accordingly, South Korea further increased foreign exchange reserves and sharply reduced its short-term debt. But the business sector's investment expenditures remained nearly stagnant, growth rate declined by nearly half, private sector and household indebtedness reached a level that is much higher than the OECD average, and further weakening of domestic demand turned into a source of high risk in terms of the country's rising export dependence under ravaging competition from China.

The nonsynchronous economic and political development has caused a fragmentation and drift in the entitlement of social rights. The social policy and IRs drifted between universalization of social rights and increasing income inequality in the entire post-1980 process and between equal rises in real wages than productivity, much higher wages and productivity, and much lower wages than productivity in the first, second, and third periods, respectively. This drift illustrates the lack of systematic economic governance and a credible commitment between the state, business, and society, which are the key requirements of erecting complementarity-based systemic governance in democratic societies.

Similarly, the enduring fragmentation of industrial governance in the absence of a systemic governance model has resulted in a drift of sectoral development in the country. In this sense, first, the shift away from rapidly growing manufacturing toward the slow-growing services sector with economic maturation has become one of the key reasons for the slowdown in the country's economic growth. Second, rising information asymmetry in the size and sectoral composition of real investment caused excessive and duplicative investment in certain industrial areas, causing declining profitability and large corporate insolvencies. In addition, coordination failures in R&D and educational strategies have resulted in (i) underperformance in generating higher output in terms of patents, scientific results, and new products, and (ii) huge skills gap and rising structural unemployment due to the declining share of vocational education and on-the-job training.

Overall, the evolution of the country's institutional stock has been managed with reactionary policy strategies to the crises of the late 1970s, 1997, and 2008. Consequent is floating policy choices between structural adjustment and discretionary activism in economic policy, between universalism and residualism in social policy, and uncontrolled domestic and external deregulation of financial, commercial, and corporate governance. Thus, the post-1980 period, in essence, first turns out to be a period of nonsynchronous economic and political development under the aegis of unbridled institutional transplantation and, therefore, second, there lingers coordinational efficiency between governments, bureaucrats, political parties, and private sector in G&D, despite the increasing initiatives in erecting a network state. It is untenable to come to such a conclusion that, during the post-1980 period, the country formulated and implemented its own institutional stock on the basis of its idiosyncratic long-term G&D targets and covered negative externalities of business cycles without deranging the systemic coherence of this ordered stock. For this reason, the country today faces an institutional trap of low growth, worsening income inequality, and slackening industrial sophistication, and is therefore unable to create systemic governance to turn its institutional stock again into a PICs-dominated one.

Presently, while on one hand there is no room for the country to erect institutional system of governance under the unifying power of an authoritarian rule, on the other, South Korea is also unable to erect such governance on the basis of credible commitment between the state, market, and society in the absence of an experience of a substantive democracy. South Korean policymakers did not utilize *formal democracy* as an opportunity for turning the authoritarian governance of the 1960s and the 1970s into a democratic pattern while keeping the former's PICs such as well-functioning economic governance. Rather, they used democracy to buy necessary time for perpetuating their short-run power by developing rent-seeking ties with *chaebols* and adapting to the international financial and economic order at the cost of debilitating the country's long-term development potential. Underlying this flawed rationality in selecting reactionary institutional strategies was, as elaborated above, a political system driven by bureaucrats under the rule of presidents rather than by political parties, lingering coherence between governments and bureaucrats in making public policy, and growing intragovernment dispute in selecting G&D strategies.

References

Ahrens, J. (2002). *Governance and Economic Development: A Comparative Institutional Approach*. Cheltenham: Edward Elgar.

Bae, J. (2001). Incentive Structure and Its Changes in the Korean Industrial Policy Regimes from 1962–1997. *The Journal of the Korean Economy, 2*(2), 297–331.

Bank of Korea (BOK). (2013). *Monetary Policy in Korea*. Seoul: BOK.

Bank of Korea (BOK). (2016). *The Korean Economy*. Seoul: BOK.

Chaibong, H. (2008). South Korea's Miraculous Democracy. *Journal of Democracy, 19*(3), 128–142.

Chang, H. (1996). *The Political Economy of Industrial Policy*. Basingstoke: Palgrave Macmillan.

Chang, S. (2003). *Financial Crisis and Transformation of Korean Business Groups*. Cambridge: Cambridge University Press.

Chang, H., Park, H., & Yoo, C. G. (2001). Interpreting the Korean Crisis: Financial Liberalization, Industrial Policy and Corporate Governance. In H. Chang, G. Palma, & D. H. Whittaker (Eds.), *Financial Liberalization and the Asian Crisis* (pp. 140–155). Basingstoke: Palgrave.

Cheery, J. (2005). Big Deal or Big Disappointment? The Continuing Evolution of the South Korean Developmental State. *Pacific Review, 18*(3), 327–354.

Cho, D. (2015). *Growth, Crisis and the Korean Economy*. Oxon: Routledge.

Chung, S., & Shu, J. (2007). Harnessing the Potential of Science and Technology. In J. Suh & D. H. Chen (Eds.), *Korea as a Knowledge Economy* (pp. 135–166). Washington, DC: The World Bank.

Claessens, S., Djankov, S., & Lang, L. (2000). The Separation of Ownership and Control in East Asian Corporations. *Journal of Financial Economics, 58*, 81–112.

Delury, G. E., & Kaple, D. A. (2006). *World Encyclopedia of Political Systems and Parties*. New York: Facts and File.

Di Maio, M. (2009). Industrial Policies in Developing Countries: History and Perspectives. In M. Cimoli, G. Dosi, & J. E. Stiglitz (Eds.), *Industrial Policy and Development: The Political Economy of Capabilities Accumulation* (pp. 108–138). Oxford: Oxford University Press.

Eichengreen, B., Perkings, D. H., & Shin, K. (2012). *From Miracle to Maturity: The Growth of the Korean Economy*. Cambridge, MA: Harvard University Press.

Fan, J. P. H., & Wong, T. J. (2005). Do External Auditors Perform a Corporate Governance Role in Emergence Markets? Evidence from East Asia. *Journal of Accounting Research, 43*(1), 35–72.

Fischer, S. (1998). The Asian Crisis: A View from the IMF. *Journal of International Financial Management and Accounting, 9*(2), 167–176.

Fleckenstein, T., & Lee, S. C. (2017). The Politics of Labor Market Reform in Coordinated Welfare Capitalism. *World Politics, 69*(1), 144–183.

Haggard, S., & Moon, J. (1990). Institutions and Economic Policy: Theory and a Korean Case Study. *World Politics, 42*(2), 210–237.

Haggard, S., & Moon, J. (2000). The Political Economy of the Korean Financial Crisis. *Review of International Political Economy, 78*(2), 197–218.

Hellman, O. (2014). Party System Institutionalization Without Parties: Evidence from Korea. *Journal of East Asian Studies, 14*, 53–84.

Hemmert, M. (2012). *Tiger Management: Korean Companies on World Markets*. London: Routledge.

Hundt, D. (2009). *Korea's Developmental Alliance*. London: Routledge.

IMF. (2017). *Financial Statistics*. Retrieved July 5, 2017, from http://data.imf.org/?sk=5477AD05-460D-4C91-9690-11E99B1ED935&sId=1390030341854

Jung, Y. (2014). Institutional Presidency and National Development. In H. Kwon & M. G. Koo (Eds.), *The Korean Government and Public Policies in Development Nexus* (pp. 11–29). Heidelberg: Springer.

Jung, J. (2015). Financial Liberalization and Institutional Incompatibility: The Unresolved Dilemma of the Korean Economy. *Politics, 35*(1), 46–57.

Kang, D. C. (2002). Bad Loans to Good Friends: Money Politics and the Developmental State in South Korea. *International Organization, 56*(1), 177–207.

Kang, N. (2010). Globalization and Institutional Change in the State-Led Model: The Case of Corporate Governance in South Korea. *New Political Economy, 15*(4), 519–542.

Kim, L. (1993). National System of Industrial Innovation: Dynamics of Capability Building in Korea. In R. Nelson (Ed.), *National Innovation Systems: A Comparative Analysis* (pp. 357–383). Oxford: Oxford University Press.

Kim, E. M. (2010a). Limits of the Authoritarian Developmental State of South Korea. In O. Edighejl (Ed.), *Constructing a Democratic Developmental State in South Africa* (pp. 97–125). Cape Town: HCR Press.

Kim, E. M., & Park, G. S. (2011). The Chaebol. In B. K. Kim & E. Vogel (Eds.), *The Park Chung-Hee Era: The Transformation of South Korea* (pp. 265–294). Cambridge, MA: Harvard University Press.

Kim, S., & Yang, D. (2011). Managing Capital Flows: The Case of the Republic of Korea. In M. Kawai & M. B. Lamberte (Eds.), *Managing Capital Flows: The Search for a Framework* (pp. 280–304). Cheltenham: Edward Elgar.

Kim, Y. (2010b). Institutions of Interest Representation and the Welfare State in Post-Democratization Korea. *Asian Perspective, 34*(1), 159–189.

Kong, T. Y. (2012). Neoliberal Restructuring in South Korea Before and After the Crisis. In C. Kyung-Sup, B. Fine, & L. Weiss (Eds.), *Developmental Politics in Transition: Neoliberal Era and Beyond* (pp. 235–253). Basingstoke: Palgrave.

Kong, T. Y. (2013). Between Late-Industrialization and Globalization: The Hybridization of Labour Relations Among Leading South Korean Firms. *New Political Economy, 18*(5), 625–652.

Koo, A. (2013). Evolution of Industrial Policies and Economic Growth in Korea: Challenges, Crises and Responses. *European Review of Industrial Economics and Policy, 7*, 1–18.

Korea Labor Institute. (2017). *Labor Statistics Archive.* Retrieved April 15, 2017, from https://www.kli.re.kr/kli_eng/selectBbsNttList.do?bbsNo=35&key=381

Larson, J. F., & Park, J. (2014). From Developmental to Network State: Government Restructuring and ICT-Led Innovation in Korea. *Telecommunications Policy, 38*, 344–359.

Lee, C. H. (1992). The Government, Financial System, and Large Private Enterprises in the Economic Development in South Korea. *World Development, 20*(2), 187–197.

Lee, Y. (2000). The Failure of the Weak State in Economic Liberalization: Liberalization, Democratization and the Financial Crisis in South Korea. *The Pacific Review, 13*(1), 115–131.

Lee, W., & Lee, B. (2003). Korean Industrial Relations in the Era of Globalization. *Journal of Industrial Relations, 45*(4), 505–520.

Lee, C. H., Lee, K., & Lee, K. (2002). Chaebols, Financial Liberalization and Economic Crisis: Transformation of Quasi-Internal Organization in Korea. *Asian Economic Journal, 16*(1), 17–35.

McKay, J. (2003). The Restructuring of the Korean Economy Since 1986 and the Onset of the Financial Crisis. In M. Tcha & C. Shu (Eds.), *The Korean Economy at the Crossroads* (pp. 69–83). London: Routledge.

Mo, J., & Weingast, B. R. (2013). *Korean Political and Economic Development: Crisis, Security, and Institutional Rebalancing.* Cambridge, MA: Harvard University Press.

OECD. (2000). *Pushing Ahead with Reform in Korea: Labour Market and Social Safety Net.* Paris: OECD.

OECD. (2010). *Learning for Jobs.* Paris: OECD.

OECD. (2016). *OECD Science, Technology and Innovation Outlook, Country Profile.* Korea, Paris: OECD.

OECD. (2017). *OECD Statistical Extracts.* Retrieved June 8, 2017, from http://stats.oecd.org/

Park, C. H. (2012). South Korea. In T. Inoguchi & J. Blondel (Eds.), *Political Parties and Democracy: Contemporary Western Europe and Asia* (pp. 127–142). Palgrave: Basingstoke.

Park, S., & Koo, Y. (2013). Innovation-Driven Cluster Development Strategies in Korea. *European Review of Industrial Economics and Policy, 5*, 1–17.

Peng, I., & Wong, J. (2008). Institutions and Institutional Purpose: Continuity and Change in East Asian Social Policy. *Politics & Society, 26*(1), 61–88.

Pirie, I. (2005). The Korean State. *New Political Economy, 10*(1), 25–42.

Pirie, I. (2015). Korea and the Global Economic Crisis. *The Pacific Review, 29*(5), 671–692.

Schüller, M., Conlé, M., & Shim, D. (2012). Korean Innovation Governance Under Lee Myung-Bak—A Critical Analysis of Governmental Actors' New Division of Labour. In J. Mahlich & W. Pascha (Eds.), *Korean Science and Technology in an International Perspective* (pp. 109–128). Heidelberg: Springer-Verlag.

Shin, J. (2014). *The Global Financial Crisis and the Korean Economy*. London: Routledge.

Shin, J., & Chang, H. (2003). *Restructuring Korea Inc*. London: Routledge.

Shin, J., & Chang, H. (2005). Economic Reform After the Financial Crisis: A Critical Assessment of Institutional Transition and Transition Costs in South Korea. *Review of International Political Economy, 12*(3), 409–433.

Song, B. N. (1990). *The Rise of the Korean Economy*. New York: Oxford University Press.

Tsutsumi, M. Jones, R. S., & Cargill, T. F. (2010). *The Korean Financial System: Overcoming the Global Financial Crisis and Addressing Remaining Problems*. OECD Economics Department Working Papers 796, OECD, Paris.

Uttam, J. (2012). Korea's New Techno-Scientific Strategy: Realigning State, Market and Society. In J. Mahlich & W. Pascha (Eds.), *Korean Science and Technology in International Perspective* (pp. 41–62). Berlin: Springer-Verlag.

Wade, R. (1998). The Asian Debt-and-Development Crisis of 1997-?: Causes and Consequences. *World Development, 26*(8), 1535–1553.

Witt, M. A. (2014). South Korea: Plutocratic State-Led Capitalism Reconfiguring. In M. Witt & G. Redding (Eds.), *The Oxford Handbook of Asian Business Systems* (pp. 216–237). Oxford: Oxford University Press.

Woo, J. (1991). *Race to the Swift: State and Finance in Korean Industrialization*. New York: Columbia University Press.

World Bank. (2017). *World Development Indicators*. Retrieved July 13, 2017, from http://databank.worldbank.org/data/reports.aspx?source=world-development-indicators

Yang, J. (2010). Korean Social Concertation at the Crossroads: Consolidation and Deterioration? *Asian Survey, 50*(3), 449–473.

Yang, J. (2013). Parochial Welfare Politics and the Small: Welfare State in South Korea. *Comparative Politics, 45*(4), 457–475.

Yim, S. D. (2005). *Korea's National Innovation System and Science and Technology Policy*. Seoul: Science and Technology Policy Institute.

4

Neither by State Nor by Market: The Turkish Case

Abstract This chapter examines Turkey's development experience in the period 1960–2017 using the analytic frame suggested in Chap. 1. In doing so, the chapter reaches four interrelated conclusions. The first is that a development strategy drawn upon reactive reorientations between state- and market-led recipes rather than upon a systemic governance is bound to result in institutional fragmentation. The second is that enduring institutional fragmentation drags a country's economic development into a process of drift. The third is that the process of institutional drift not only produces structural imperfections but also paralyzes emerging reform initiatives. Finally, the fourth is that a reform of developmental institutions cannot reach success without taking into account of systemic complications of the negative and positive institutional complementarities.

Keywords Turkey • Growth • Development • Institutions • Complementarity • Governance

© The Author(s) 2018
T. Akan, *The Complementary Roots of Growth and Development*,
https://doi.org/10.1007/978-3-319-68932-6_4

4.1   Introduction

As an upper-income developing country, Turkey applied an inward-looking import-substitutionist strategy in the 1960s and 1970s, which resulted in a balance of account crisis in the late 1970s. The country then adopted a neoliberal strategy under the guidance of the IMF and World Bank beginning on 24 January 1980 (the Turkish economy was managed through IMF standby agreements over 16 of the 37 following years).

After experiencing catastrophic financial crises in 1994 and 2001 and then pursuing strict austerity measures in particular from April 2001 onward, the country now faces institutional challenges in contriving viable transition strategies from an efficiency-driven economic structure to an innovation-driven one. On one hand, the Turkish state has embarked on entrepreneurial initiatives such as creating a national automobile brand under the direct leadership of the Turkish Research Agency (a public institution) with the early 2010s in view of the abstention of the private sector from undertaking such entrepreneurial risks. On the other hand, the country maintains a strict austerity strategy and does not intend to adopt a protectionist position with a weighted tariff rate, 2.1 percent, lower than the OECD average, 2.3 percent, for the period of 2000–2013 (World Bank 2015a).

This chapter is organized into three sections. In the first section, Turkey's developmental adventure of 1960–2015 is examined in terms of the evolutionary dynamics of its political and bureaucratic architecture, economic policies, corporate governance structure, and industrial and institutional performance. In the second section, the institutional fragmentation of the country's G&D process is disentangled in the context of NICs and PICs of the country's institutional stock. Finally, in the third section, the chapter investigates the institutional trap facing the country in achieving a transformation from an efficiency-driven to an innovation-driven economic structure.

4.2   The Political Roots of Ideologic Balkanization

Turkey employs a secular republican political regime established in 1923 that has descended from Ottoman Islam. In its current form, this regime has been polarized between etatist secularism, civic Islam, and political democracy, dating back to institutional renewals in the Empire since the early nineteenth century (Berkes 1964). Between 1960 and 2015, as Table 4.1 shows, this dissident landscape precipitated an enduring political fragmentation, though not in the periods 1966–1971, 1983–1991, and 2003–2015, which manifested as short-lived coalition governmental periods among ideologically segregated parties. This political schism precluded the erection of a durable and substantive democratic system. Rather, the institutional underpinnings of these periods from reactive economic policies to the constitutions of 1961 and 1982 were shaped by the military coup d'états of May 1960 and September 1980. Furthermore, the democratically elected governments of 1960–2015 perpetuated these economic policies and could not make even civic constitutions to end enduring military tutelage over civic politics. Despite the incessant power of the Justice and Development Party (AKP) from 2002 to 2017, Turkey's Constitution of 1982 remains in force with the exception of certain major amendments, and the composition of the Turkish parliament following the November 2015 general elections demonstrates that it will remain in force during the next legislative session of 2015–2019 due to an unremitting schism between political parties represented in the parliament.

Ideological clashes between political battlegrounds have caused clientelistic rather than meritocratic rules to determine the career paths of bureaucratic cadres. The reshuffling of these cadres during the incumbency of each new government, quite contrary to the Weberian merit-based and durable tradition of bureaucracy, precluded the designing, enforcing, and revising of Turkish development plans beyond conjunctural encounters. A striking example pertains to a declaration made by the Minister of Justice of the SHP-DYP coalition government in 1995, Mehmet Moğultay: 'Yes, five thousand personnel cadres had been allocated to my ministry to be employed by exam. Should I have given these cadres to the nationalists instead of my organization's members?' (NTV 2015).

As even admitted by the leader of the AKP, Recep Tayyip Erdoğan, the AKP governments of 2002–2013 collaborated with the Gülen Movement, thought to be a religious sect at that time. Apparently, this collaboration aimed to counteract similar initiatives by previous governments. Quite perplexingly, it turned out that the so-called Movement, now entitled Gulen Terrorist Organization (FETO), had infiltrated the Turkish state in

Table 4.1 The incumbent parties in Turkey, 1960–2017

Incumbent parties	Inter.	CHP		CHP-CKMP	CHP	Indep	AP	Inter.	Indep.	CHP	Indep	AP-MSP	CHP	AP-MSP	CHP	AP
	AP			YP-Indep.						MSP		MP-CGP		MHP	Indep.	
Duration of incumbency	May	Dec.	Jun.	Dec.	Feb.	Oct.	Mar.	May	Jan.	Nov.	Mar.	Jun.	July	Jan.	Nov.	Sep.
	1960	1961	1962	1963	1964	1965	1966–1971	1972	1973	1974	1975	1976	1977	1978	1979	1980

Incumbent parties		ANAP	DYP-SHP	DYP-	ANAP	RP	ANAP-DSP	DSP	DSP-MHP	AKP
				CHP	DYP	DYP	DTP-Ind.		- ANAP	
Duration of incumbency	Dec.	Nov.	Oct.	Mar.	Jun.	Jun	Jan	May	Nov.	
	1980	1981-83	1984-91	1991-95	1996	1997	1998	1999	2000-01	2002-

The ideology of major political parties in Turkey

Secular etatist or Kemalist social democrat	CHP (1923), SHP (1985–95), and DSP (1985)
Conservative liberal	DP (1946–1960) and ANAP (1982)
Secular liberal	AP (1961–80) and DYP (1983-2007)
Turkish nationalist	MHP (1969)
Islamic	MNP-MSP-RP-FP-SP (1970, 1972, 1983, 1997, 2001)
Conservative democrat	AKP (2002)

a massive scale. It then initiated a failed but bloody coup d'état in February 2016, martyring 248 Turkish citizens by using barbarian methods such as hitting them with warplanes and shooting them with guns.

It is the Civil Servants Act of 1965 that is still in force with ad hoc amendments that regulates the legal status of high- and low-ranking Turkish bureaucracy. The Act aims to recruit a submissive and loyal class of civil servants and bureaucracy, which serve as the main criteria of selection and promotion. Middle- and high-ranking bureaucrats in the public sector were selected through a written and verbal exam created by the recruiting agency or ministry. It was the verbal exam and not the written exam that determined who should be selected. From 1999 onward, public personnel have been selected based on an objective exam, the KPSS, which was created by a central selection and placement organization, the OSYM. However, as the verbal exams are used, the same order can be suggested to take its place particularly for high-ranking bureaucrats. Furthermore, it has recently been revealed that the FETO had stolen the questions of these exams and thus systematically placed its member militants in certain state institutions.

The Special Expert Commission Report on the Improvement of Public Administration describes the institutional imperfections in the selection and promotion of bureaucratic cadres in the following way:

> The education, success and professional capabilities are not reckoned with during the recruitment of low- or high-ranking staff for public sector institutions. This results in the inefficiency of service quality… In the public sector, wage policy is determined in a static manner according to employment status but not based on a progressive or regressive scale dependent upon success, qualification and performance criteria. In our country, a centralist, etatist and proceduralist culture of administration has been prevalent, dating back to the Tanzimat of 1839. (TKB 2000: 52–56)

The significance of this report lies in the fact that it reflects the common view of a wide array of participants ranging from business and employer organizations to academics and bureaucrats themselves and also in the fact that it was commissioned and published by the Turkish Ministry of Development (TKB) as a supplement to the Eighth Five-Year Development Plan of 2001–2005.

The Turkish state set out to clear the above-noted imperfections, having accumulated until the end of the twentieth century, through the privatization of state-owned enterprises (SOEs), the establishment of Independent Regulatory Agencies such as the Banking Regulation and Supervision Agency (1999) and Public Procurement Agency (2002), as well as the adaptation of major principles of new public management systems such as citizen orientedness, accountability, inclusive governance, performance criteria, and transparency. The neoliberal content of these reforms was such that the TKB projected the formation of public sector strategies through the prioritization of market culture and business administration over public administration (TKB 2007; TKB 2014a: 40–44).

The analysis of the country's G&D performance over the past one and a half decades presented in the following sections of this research will show that such types of theoretical suggestions to be implemented by a state-led institutional design have yet to contribute to the development of a structural change in the country's bureaucratic structure, at least in terms of conducting G&D strategies. The following statement made by the Ministry of Development in the Five-Year Plan for 2014–2018 effectively conveys this fact beforehand:

> Excessive proceduralism distorts the bureaucratic conduct from its ultimate purpose… As a result, public personnel and managers intend to comply with procedures by adapting a passive stance in perpetuating the established order rather than taking any reformist initiative. (TKB 2014b: 40)

4.3 Economic Policymaking in Successive Reactions: Developmentalism, Neoliberalism, and Austerity

The period of 1960–2015 in Turkey can be divided into three main phases in terms of economic policymaking: the import substitutionism of 1960–1979, etatist neoliberalism of 1980–2002, and the neoliberal austerity of 2003–2015. What features strategic change at each period is a reaction to the failure in the previous one. For example, Kepenek (2008: 145–146) critically emphasizes that neither the bureaucracy nor the industrial entrepreneurs were equipped for a sharp change toward an inward-looking import-substitutionist regime in the early 1960s beginning with the coup d'etat of May 1960. The leader cadre of the military junta came from the positivist segments of society and was sympathetic to socialism. General Gürsel, as the head of the junta and the then President of Turkey, declared: 'Turkey needed social reforms and socialism could be regarded as a possible avenue for development' (Karpat 2004: 48). The main reason was that the outward-looking import-substitutionist strategy adapted by the conservative liberal Democrat Party governments of 1950–1960 ended up with rising current account deficit, quadrupling inflation, and remarkable declines in public sector wages and salaries in the late 1950s.

The economic policy strategy employed between 1960 and 1979, in broad strokes, aimed to produce import goods, chiefly consumer goods and consumer durables, in the country by national enterprises or national-foreign capital partnerships. These enterprises were, in terms of main inputs, especially technology and energy, dependent on foreign markets and thrived under state's incentives including the contracts for key public sector projects. In this context, the SOEs turned their mission from consumer goods production to intermediate goods industries in the post-1950 period, providing subsidized inputs to the private industry. In addition, Turkish planners chose to place ceilings on key relative prices including the exchange rate, nominal interest rates, and the product prices of the SOEs. The overvalued exchange rates and negative interest rates retarded a potential increase in exports and private savings, respectively. At the end of the period, this caused a drastic balance of account crises. The vicious circle was *more import for more production, more foreign exchange for more import, and more borrowing for more foreign exchange*. Thus, the state's nonreciprocal provision of direct and indirect subsidies resulted in the burdening of the cost by the public sector along with the embedding of a leisure *class* of businessmen (Öniş 1998: 497–498; Bayar 1996).

Afterward, in the period 1980–2002, the country turned toward neoliberalism with the 24 January 1980 decisions taken and enforced under IMF and the World Bank surveillance (Boratav et al. 1996). Underlying was that, by making the country's industrial establishment subservient to foreign capital, especially in intermediate goods, the state-subsidized and debt-financed model fell into a vicious circle in the late 1970s: rising balance of account and current account deficits, decreasing and negative growth rates, soaring public sector borrowing requirement (PSBR), unemployment, inflation, and interest rates. Instead of complete elimination, however, the face of state intervention changed, in this case through export subsidies ranging from direct payment to exporters through tax rebates and cash premia to preferential and subsidized export credits with a rediscount rate below commercial interest rates until the end of 1988, under the shadow of a widespread rent-seeking action.

From May 1981 onward, in this new environment, the Central Bank of Turkey (TCMB) began to adjust the exchange rate on a daily basis. In July 1984, domestic and external Turkish and foreign exchange transactions were substantially liberalized, and interest rates were deregulated as a structural enhancement for the development of the financial sector. In 1989, capital account was fully liberalized, and the convertibility of the Turkish Lira (TL) was recognized, allowing the sale and purchase of national or foreign currencies or securities in the country or abroad. The capital account liberalization in late 1989 has substantially changed the monetary policymaking environment, exposing the economy to strong and mainly short-term capital flows. TCMB summarizes the consequence of these *institutional rushes* in this way:

> The Turkish experience after full liberalization can be well summarized by a very familiar transmission mechanism; large public deficits, putting pressure on shallow financial sector, raise the real interest rates ending up with an increasing dependency on more short-term capital inflows. Eventually, less and less resources were available to production and investment. (TCMB 2002: 31)

The catastrophic financial crises of 1994 and 2001 led to the adaptation of an IMF austerity program entitled 'Turkey's Program for Transition to a Strong Economy', and the AKP governments of the period October 2002 to June 2015 maintained this program. The party was able to pursue strict austerity that resulted in a relatively balanced budget thanks to contractionary monetary policy, declining ratios of public sector fixed capital formation (investment), and final consumption expenditures,

Table 4.2 Major macroeconomic variables of Turkish economy, 1960–2012

Parameters	1960–1979	1980–2002	2003–2012
GDP growth	5.1	3.8	5.0
Fixed capital formation in the public sector	6.8	5.7	3.4
Consolidated budget balance/PSBR	0.9	5.9	1.9
Inflation	15.7	62	10.1
Unemployment	5.8	8.3	10.8
Current account deficit	−1.1	−0.8	−5.2

Source: TKB (2015c)

which were accompanied by steady rises in indirect taxes and very limited real increases in civil servant salaries, limited increases in average public sector employment, and, ultimately, relatively high privatization revenues, especially in 2006. There were mainly two predicaments stemming from a long-standing austerity program: the persistence of unemployment above 10 percent and the soaring current account deficits due particularly to the ongoing dependence of Turkey's industrial sector on import intermediate goods. And during this period, as in the 1980s and 1990s, current account deficits were financed by portfolio investment, predominantly short term, as a result of increased uncovered interest arbitrage in Turkey relative to emerging market economies, indicating the net return on domestic short-term financial assets.

The most prominent trend across the four subperiods, as shown in Table 4.2, is that the structural transformation between 1980 and 2002, in spite of neoclassical theory, initiated an *uncreative destruction* in systemic terms. The slackening growth with both high inflation and unemployment despite the rather high PSBR demonstrates the destructive impact of *volatile, untimely,* and *reactionary restructurations*, rather than the stabilizing impact of neoliberal policy recommendations. The persistence of unemployment and inflation with a declining public investment ratio and phenomenal current account deficit between 2003 and 2012 implies that budgetary austerity did not redound to curbing inflation and stabilizing output and employment, and austerity was not effective in the absence of strong industrial performance.

4.4   Corporate Governance: Concentrated Ownership, Market Capitalization, and Foreign Debt

As Table 4.3 illustrates, the vast majority of Turkish enterprises (roughly 80 percent in total) consist of either micro- or small- and midsized enterprises: SMEs owned by founding personnel or family. Whereas large family firms manage corporate boards, these boards are overwhelmingly dominated by family members rather than by independent or professional members. Furthermore, institutional corporations constitute a small portion of Turkey's business sector. Beyond types of businesses, the building blocks of corporate governance in Turkey, in parallel with the above-noted political and economic path dependencies, pertains to clientelistic relationships between corporate owners and public authorities, shareholder actions bounded in partaking in board meetings while not in taking an active role in managing major asset transactions, hierarchical organizational management dominated by family ties, a lack of credible nonfinancial information disclosure, the widespread sharing of asymmetric information between companies, and the weak contractual status of employees and professional managers (Ugur and Ararat 2006; Biddle and Minor 1997).

In this regard, shareholder or stakeholder capitalism has yet to be instituted in the country. The stock market capitalization of GDP in the country, 27 percent, despite being slightly higher than the average for upper-middle-income countries, 26 percent, is nearly four times lower than that of the United Kingdom and United States and is three-fifths that of the Euro area countries (World Bank 2015a). Unlike institutionalized shareholder models, Ararat (2011) finds that family-owned holding companies held majority control over 54 of the 122 companies listed on the Istanbul Stock Exchange in 2006 and 2008. Furthermore, the control rights of families reach 56 percent when all ownership stakes are combined under the control of an ultimate owner. Expectedly, this results in the nomination and election of the board members and in the determination of these firms' relations with states, banks, and employees

Table 4.3 A taxonomy of Turkish businesses

Type of business	Micro businesses	Small- and medium-sized businesses	Large family firms	Institutional corporations
Ownership	Founder	Mostly founder	Founder family	Controlling owner + shareholders
Corporate governance	Owner/manager	Owner/manager	Family board and family manager	Independent board members and professional managers
Employment rules and protection	Informal	Frequent circumvention of employment rules	Partial compliance with employment rules	Full compliance
Accuracy of wage reporting and social security contribution	–	Partial	Mostly	Fully
Size (approximate number of workers)	1–10	10–250	250–2500	2500+
Productivity (% of average productivity in 20+ firms)	10–20%	40–80%	100–120%	130–150%
Share in business sector employment	Around 45%	Between 35 and 40%	Around 15%	Around 4%
Share in manufacturing employment	Around 25%	Between 40 and 45%	Around 25%	Around 6%

Source: OECD (2014: 86)

through the control of shareholders or families to the point where, in frequent cases, CEOs are excluded from the board.

As a matter of fact, as shown in the stakeholder model of post-war Germany where workers' saving turned into long-term credits of productive enterprises through the banking system, family ownership may be expected to contribute to the long-term stability of efficiency and equity. Instead of institutionalizing their governance structures and improving their production methodologies, Turkish private firms have however remained aloof to high-risk sectors and have financed their rising productivity gap by borrowing foreign debt, by increasing downward pressure on real wages, and by aggressively de-unionizing their workplaces. Furthermore, as illustrated in Table 4.3, productivity levels are unevenly distributed among SMEs and large family firms. Taken together with the fact that the former enjoy much less owner capital, lower levels of physical capital intensity, and limited access to credit and capital markets, this uneven distribution not only distorts research allocation and free competition among these enterprises but also aggravates social inequalities in disfavor of those employees who work for the former (OECD 2014: 84).

The consequence is an ever-widening gap between real wages and labor productivity particularly from the 1980s onward and plummeting rates of trade union density, as shown at Figs. 4.1 and 4.2. The rate of annual change in real wages and labor productivity in the period 1980–2001 was 0.2 percent and 3.7 percent, respectively. The same rates were 5.4 and 3.8 percent, respectively, for the period 1961–1979 (TSI 2013: 250). In the absence of alternative workplace governance institutions such as work councils and of any regulation conditioning worker representation at company executive or decision-making boards, company owners and management teams determine employer-employee relationships in tandem with their firm's short-run objectives (Uçkan 2013). Workers participate in certain councils such as worker health and security, annual leave, and dispute resolution. However, these are procedural councils that address minor issues.

The further disqualification of stakeholder models in Turkey has served as the link between private banks, enterprises, and households. The 1990s witnessed a hot money policy of Turkish governments with high real

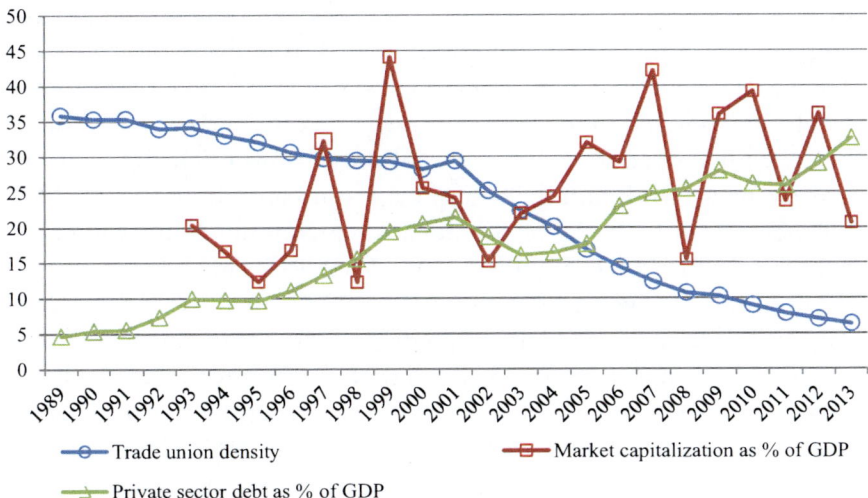

Fig. 4.1 Market capitalization, foreign debt, and trade union density in Turkey, 1988–2012. Source: World Bank (2015a), TKB (2015c)

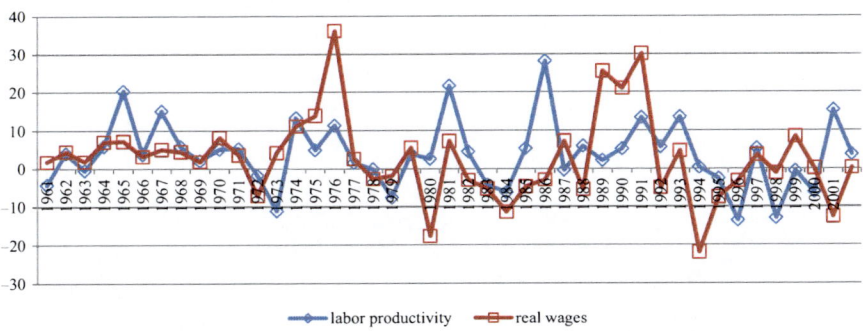

Fig. 4.2 Labor productivity and real wages in Turkish manufacturing sector, 1961–2001. Source: Author's calculations based on data provided by TSI (2013: 250)

interest rates to attract speculative capital, and this became one of the main causes of macroeconomic fragilities as the TCMB notes above. High returns on treasury bills tempted the domestic banking sector to fund large government deficits by borrowing from foreign markets to the extent that the share of government securities in Turkish bank portfolios reached 23 percent in 1999. Quite paradoxically, high interest rates in the public sector came to be the main source of net corporate profits as well. Complementing this rent-based government-private banking-real sector nexus was state banks' lending operations at below market rates to corporate and individual donors, farmers, or other electoral constituencies. In 2000, the uncompensated duty losses of these banks reached 12 percent of the country's GNP, and the cost of bankrupt banks in the 2000–2001 crisis then amounted to 50 billion dollars, representing 25 percent of the country's GDP in 2001 (Steinherr et al. 2004: 4–5, Fig. 4.3).

Re-forming arrangements from the late 1999 aimed to improve monitoring in the supervision of banking systems by incorporating market risk into capital adequacy requirements and therefore motivated banks to consolidate their positions. As a result, bank nonperforming loans retreated to 3 percent in 2014 from 29 percent in 2001. However, the banking sector's long-term investment credit level did not increase. Underlying this trend was high collateral rates and low banking sector total credit capacities in relation to the GDP, which stems from low domestic savings. The rates of domestic credits to the private sector by national banks for GDP in Turkey, the OECD, and Euro area countries were 31 percent, 85 percent, and 96 percent on average for 2000–2013.

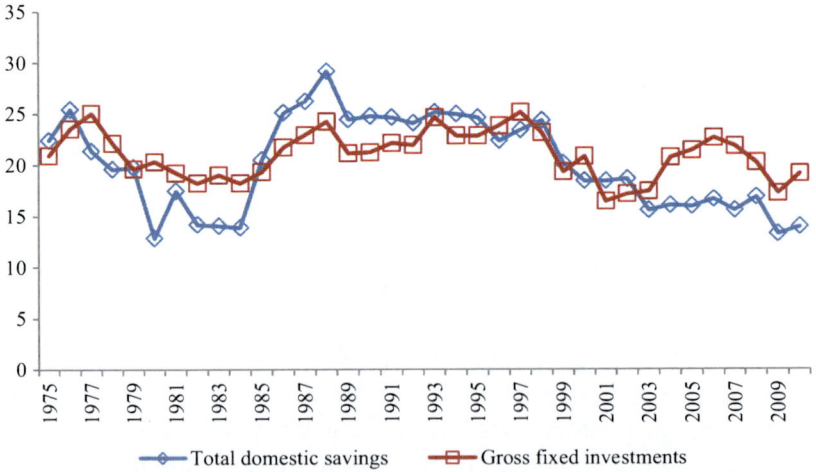

Fig. 4.3 Total domestic savings and gross fixed investments in Turkey, 1975–2010. Source: TKB (2015c)

Furthermore, the share of manufacturing firms in banking credits plummeted to approximately 20 percent in 2012 from 50 percent in the early 2000s despite the presence of mainly short maturities (BDDK 2014: 104). However, the ratio of individual credits and credit cards to total credits provided by Turkish banks jumped to 25 percent in 2013 from 12 percent in January of 2004. This has been based on the fact that the growth model in Turkey has become dependent on household debt particularly in the form of housing and credit card loans. Thus, the valuation of bank deposits for capitalizing still comparatively high real interest rates on government securities and on consumer credits has become one of the biggest barriers before the genesis of positive intercomplementarity between savings, fixed capital formation, and equal income distribution (Bakır and Öniş 2010). The plummeting rates of savings and gross fixed investments that occurred after a short-run increase between 1984 and 1988 illustrate this fact. In the early 2010s, total domestic savings in Turkey declined to the lowest rates in the country's history. Consequently, as noted above and as shown in Fig. 4.1, a soaring rate of foreign indebtedness for private sector firms resulted.

4.5   Industrial and Institutional Performance in Turkey

Imperfections in Turkey's politico-bureaucratic, economic, and corporate governance structures constrained its industrial and institutional performance to a great extent. As a result, the income gap between Turkey and the developed economies has remained roughly unchanged since World War I (Altuğ et al. 2008).

As shown in Table 4.4, although Turkey's growth performance has been slightly higher than that of the Latin American countries from the 1960s onward, it is far smaller than that of the East Asian countries and China (particularly relative to South Korea and Malaysia). This can be traced to a much higher gradual increase in China and South Korea's per capita income relative to Turkey's from 1960 to 2013. Of these two underlying factors, the first pertains to the fact that manufacturing value added in Turkey is less than two-thirds that of these countries. However, the second and more important factor relates to the fact that the Turkish

Table 4.4 Major indicators of structural change in selected countries[a]

Country	GDP growth % annual	GDP per capita growth % annual			Manufacturing value added as % of GDP	High-tech exports as % of manufactured exports	R & D expend. as % of GDP	Tariff rate, weighted mean all products, %	Government expendit. on education as % of GDP
	60–'13	60–79	80–99	00–'13	60–'13	88–'13	00–'13	88.–'13	70–'13
Turkey	4.5	3154	4842	7240	19.0	2.0	0.6	4.0	2.9
Argentina	3.0	4480	4893	6222	27.0	7.1	0.5	10.0	2.6
Brazil	4.3	2571	4065	5045	23.6	9.8	1.1	12.2	4.6
Chile	4.3	2809	4460	8045	19.2	4.1	0.4	7.6	3.6
Mexico	4.0	4667	6790	7985	20.4	16.4	0.4	8.6	4.0
Korea, Rep.	7.2	2115	8684	19,700	24.2	26.3	2.8	9.2	3.5
China	8.4	139	537	2189	33.6	18.8	1.2	14.4	1.8
Japan	3.7	14,179	28,700	35,678	22.2	23.3	3.2	13.7	4.2
Germany	2.1	19,972	27,841	36,138	22.8	14.9	2.5	3.0	4.7
United States	3.0	21,016	32,114	43,597	14.9	29.1	2.6	2.5	5.1

Source: World Development Indicators (2015a)

[a](') refers to 2000s

economy lags far behind in the proportion of high-tech products in man-ufactured exports. This rate for the Turkish economy is infinitesimal even compared to the Latin American countries.

In fact, there has been a remarkable structural change in the Turkish manufacturing sector. The country's medium-high-tech exports increased from 14 percent in the 1980s to 26 percent in the 2000s on average. Over the same period, however, manufacturing exports became strictly dependent on the importation of middle-high and high-tech products, predominantly of intermediate machinery and equipment, at a rate of 65 percent. The severity of this dependence and of its deficit-creating impacts over the current account balance can be seen in Table 4.5, which shows the country's performance in export and import rates of medium-high and high-tech products relative to upper-middle-income Mexico and high-income Korea in the period 1995–2009 (OECD 2015a).

Along with macro institutional factors such as politico-bureaucratic structures and corporate governance, Turkey's poor performance in manag-ing industrial governance institutions and micro institutional factors of education and training, R&D, and incentive systems retards the country's transition to an innovation-driven structure. According to the Global Competitiveness Index (GCI), the country's ranking in sub-parameters from poor to the worst is those that are of determinant value in transition from an efficient to innovation-driven economy: the quality of scientific institutions, the availability of scientists and engineers, university-industry collaboration in R&D, capacities for innovation, and finally company spending on R&D (WEF 2015). As shown in Table 4.4, the country's R&D expenditures, albeit being higher than those of Argentina, Chile, and Mexico, are half of those of Brazil and China and are roughly one-fourth to one-fifth than those of the United States, Germany, South Korea, and Japan. In addition, the share of the private sector in R&D expenditures increased to only 48 percent of GDP in 2013 from 27 percent in 1990.

Table 4.5 Medium-high and high-tech exports and imports in Turkey, Mexico, and South Korea, 1995–2009

	Turkey	Mexico	Korea
Export	29.7	74.4	69.6
Import	50.7	61.8	46.8

Source: OECD (2015a)

Expectedly, in the GCI, Turkey's position in innovation has receded from 51st in 2006–2007 to 56th in 2014–2015 (WEF 2006, 2015). As a corollary, governmental expenditures on education in Turkey are remarkably lower than those of the countries shown in Table 4.4, with the exception of those of China and Brazil. As a result, the labor force with a tertiary education in the country has been roughly two to three times smaller than those of East Asia, the United States, the United Kingdom, Japan, and the LACs (with the exception of Brazil) from the 1990s onward. As another indicator of the state of the qualified labor force, in the GCI, the country's rank in terms of the availability of scientists and engineers retreated from 44 to 59 from 2006–2007 to 2014–2015, respectively. Furthermore, according to PISA indicators on international student assessment, the performance of Turkish students at the age of 15 in science and math (468 and 443, respectively) is far lower than the OECD average of 500 and 488, respectively (OECD 2015b, c).

In addition to the nonstrategic management of education, the labor force, research, and innovation, the country's incentive policy has also evolved into a negative complementary in its comparatively poor performance in industrial sophistication. With the inauguration of the State Planning Organization (SPO) in 1960, Turkey launched a number of incentives related to the provision of cheap input and credit, tax facilities, import quotas, and high customs duties. Furthermore, during the post-1980 period, incentives were applied on a selective basis for prioritized sectors specified in development plans and were renewed annually. However, during the second half of the 1990s, the selective incentive system was discontinued. A watershed in this regard was related to the fact that in 2003, to clarify complications in the implementation of frequently changed incentive regulations, the investment discount was flattened to 40 percent for all sectors and regions rather than being diversified for each sector and region. An indicator of the country's nonstrategic management of industrial incentives pertains to the fact that these incentives were granted predominantly to low and middle-low technology sectors. In 1980 and 2008, middle-high and high-technology sectors constituted 30 percent and 1 percent of total investment incentives, respectively (Eser 2011; Yavan 2011).

On the other hand, the lack of effective industrial governance can be suggested to have played a significant role in the country's nonsystemic management of incentives, in processes of industrial sophistication, in education quality and labor force supply, and in the manifestation of relatively lower growth performance. This ineffectiveness can be traced through the preparation and implementation of Turkish five-year development plans by the TKB and earlier on by the SPO. Table 4.6 shows how the plans were prepared and executed by a hierarchy of state organizations in the 1960s.

During the preparation of the plans, SOEs' managers were widely consulted, whereas the private sector was relevant only through indirect instruments such as subsidies (Çiller 1972: 76–83). A positive development that occurred during the plan preparation period was the formation of special expert commissions (SECs) that commenced with the seventh

Table 4.6 The preparatory stages of Turkish development plans in the 1960s

First stage	Second stage	Third stage
1-Central planning department (CPD) aggregates data from the past and makes preliminary projections	5-Central Planning Organization makes macro projections, sectoral projections, and project evaluations	9-The SPO prepares the final draft
2-CPD projects various growth rates at the macroeconomic level	6-HPC examines the project proposals	10-HPC is consulted
3-High Planning Council (HPC) chooses best variant and determines strategy	7-Foreign stakeholders are consulted (economists, authorities, and international organizations)	11-Cabinet approves
4-Cabinet makes the final decision	8-The State Planning Organization (SPO) changed to the TKB in 2011, revises the sectoral and macro projections	12-SPO approves 13-SPO prepares yearly programs and budgets according to the plan 14-Coordination Division executes and controls the plan and makes periodic reports on the implementation of the plan which are reviewed by the Cabinet

Source: Çiller (1972: 83)

development plan of 1996–2000. However, nongovernmental stakeholders provided only consultation and did not play active role in monitoring enforcement processes or in revising the targets annually or biannually. What illustrates the static nature of developmental governance in the country is that in its institutional strategic plan of 2014, the TKB notes that 'a system will be designed to periodically monitor and evaluate the development plans' (TKB 2014c: 26). It is quite perplexing that an organization of 55 years has now become aware of such a vital requirement.

Other firm evidence of the fact that Turkey has yet to adapt effective developmental governance relates to the industrial policy expectations of major sector representatives contributing to the preparation of the Special Commission Report on the Transformation of the Manufacturing Sector in Turkey (see Table 4.7). These expectations, which call for a systemic

Table 4.7 Industrial policy expectations of major sectors in Turkey

Domestic products should be prioritized by both central and local administrations (by pharmaceuticals, automotive, and electronic industry)	As the current account balance grows due to the lack of a systematic pricing strategy in favor of domestic producers, there are compelling and precise measures to be implemented in this area (by ceramic industry)
Facilitating the inclusion of domestic products in repayment schemes in the face of the import goods (by medical devices sector)	Offset should be made compulsory particularly for big and foreign financed public projects (by machine industry)
At least one year before public procurements, the plan, program, and the content of the procurement should be declared to the domestic producers to enable them to develop products for these procurements and to compete with the international producers (by electronic industry)	As the SMEs are unable to take part in big-sized procurements, these procurements should be broken down into a few parts and a certain amount be allocated to the SMEs (by furniture industry)
A process of assessment for quality and price should be conducted in public procurement, and the domestic industry should be oriented to innovation (there is already 15 percent price advantage according to the Public Procurement Act numbered 4734) (by textile-garment and leather industry)	

TKB (2014d: 30–31)

governance strategy between the state and market in achieving industrial sophistication, were those that Taiwan effectively implemented in as early as the 1960s (see Wade 1990).

4.6   The Institutional Fragmentation in Turkey's Developmental Experience

NICs in Turkish Developmental Governance

In this subsection, Turkey's developmental institutional stock is examined mainly with reference to its macro NICs and PICs. The micro ones are examined in terms of their contributions to the genesis and embedding of the macro ones.

Table 4.8 illustrates macro (systemic) and micro (subsystemic) NICs in Turkish PE. The first macro NIC of Turkish PE pertains to its actors' *fragmented identity* arising out of pronounced political and bureaucratic balkanization in the public sector. The short-lived coalition governments of 1960–2002 aggravated and extended this balkanization over state-business relations. In turn, owner- and family-dominated enterprises thrived under the protection of governments with which they enjoyed either a patronage or an ideological affiliation particularly from the early 1930s to the late 1970s. Albeit partly rationalized with the 2001 financial crisis, such a shallow capitalist rational between commodified Islamic normativity and reactionist secular radicalism still holds sway over state-business relations in contemporary Turkey.

This fragmented identity held back the genesis of a *self-reinforcing rational* among its actors as the second macro NIC that would otherwise underlie the determination and pursuance of a workable long-term development strategy in consideration of the evolutionary complications of the country's factor endowments and institutional qualifications. The fact that the members of short-lived governments have always monopolized strategy-forming councils such as the High Planning Board prevented bureaucrats from taking initiative in determining or pursuing long-term developmental goals in the face of short-run opportunist or divergent political interventions. Instead, Turkish bureaucracy has been used to

Table 4.8 The NICs in Turkish Developmental Governance, 1960–2010

Macro – Systemic NICs	Fragmented identity	Lack of self-reinforcing rationality	Over-autonomous state	Developmental rush	Institutional trap
Micro NICs in public sector	Political and bureaucratic balkanization	Floating policy adaptations and proceduralism	Sharp institutional breaks, regulatory fragmentation, and high transformation costs	Supply-side taxation, authoritarian labor laws, palliative social policy, low expenditure on and ideological management of education system	Comparatively lower economic growth, dependence on foreign savings and on imported intermediate goods, faltering industrial sophistication, high inequality of income, and high structural unemployment
Micro NICs in private sector and socio economic structure	Shallow capitalist rationality and patronage-based business-making	Weak industrial clustering in wage setting, workforce training, and technology creation	Asymmetric information, high transaction costs, and ad hoc investment decisions	Exclusive governance, wage restraint, commodificatory sub contracting, and high level of informal employment	Limited credible commitment between state, market, and society, limited educational investment by the households, inadequate stock of qualified labor force, and low rate of labor force participation

(continued)

Table 4.8 (continued)

The NICs and PICs, 2010–2015*

Macro – Systemic NICs and PICs	Fragmented identity	Thriving capacity of self-reinforcing rationality	Burgeoning entrepreneurial state	Rising rationale of intercomplementary transformation	Institutional trap
Micro NICs and PICs in public sector	Political and bureaucratic balkanization	Relative political stability and ongoing institutional improvements	Taking initiative in transforming dependent institutional and industrial structure	Priority Transformation Programs	Comparatively lower economic growth, dependence on foreign savings and on imported intermediate goods, faltering industrial sophistication, high inequality of income, and high structural unemployment
Micro NICs and PICs in private sector and socio economics	Shallow capitalist rationality and patronage-based business-making	Weak industrial clustering in wage setting, workforce training, and technology creation	Asymmetric information, high transaction costs, and ad hoc investment decisions	Exclusive governance, wage restraint, sub contracting, and high level of informal employment	Limited credible commitment between state, market, and society, limited educational investment by the households, inadequate stock of qualified labor force, and low rate of labor force participation

*Gray areas stand for the PICs.

carry out the procedural transactions of floating developmental policies. With this lack of a strategic pathway of development, Turkish business-men did not become part of a state-led development strategy under a working governance regime; did not establish industrial clusters or collaborate in wage setting, workforce training, and technology genera-tion; and did not venture into a progressive liberal or capitalist strategy and compel political parties or bureaucracies to adopt this strategy.

Instead of undertaking optimal regulatory discretion in cooperation with nongovernmental actors, an *overautonomous state* as the third macro NIC always determined development strategies via reactive institutional designs. This has led to the management of developmental strategies under the shadow of sharp institutional breaks by way of developmental-ism, neoliberalism, and austerity, respectively. Such a nonstrategic path-way precipitated regulatory fragmentation between over- and under-regulation beginning in the 1960s and then in the 1980s, and this resulted in financial turmoil with the 1990s in the aftermath of the full liberalization of financial markets. Faltering flows of the country's institu-tional stock and consequent unpredictability precluded the development of a rationale of strategic sector management and inter-business clusters through timely shared symmetric information between state and busi-ness. In the absence of this informational background, private enterprises opted for investing in low- or middle-technology sectors via imported intermediate goods but did not initiate micro reforms by developing an innovative organizational model or a progressive R&D policy to produce these goods within the country or to upgrade their technological endow-ment in competitive dialectics with foreign firms.

What has made this leisured strategy chronic is that the state oversub-sidized the private sector through incentives that were selective or unselec-tive during random periods but that were not contingent on productive performance in nearly all periods. With this lack of a long-term strategy of development, Turkish state did not invest in direct production in upper-middle or high-tech sectors, and it did not compel the private sec-tor to do so through performance-contingent incentives such as guaran-teed public procurement. Instead, Turkey first depleted its internal resources for creating an un-innovative stock of entrepreneurs, picking the leisure, during the 1960s and 1970s. The country then paid excessive transformation costs arising out of the adaptation problems of these enterprises to the global value chain from the 1980s onward. An underlying factor has been the country's obsession with a *static* strategy of development over a systemic governance strategy in flexibly managing the dialectics of NICs and PICs according to changing constraints and opportunities in time.

The Turkish state's overautonomy in governing the country's institutional development is essentially derived from the socioeconomic demands of labor and civic organizations. This overautonomy has been designed to immediately enforce developmental goals by refraining equity input from being incorporated into the country's governance processes. This approach can be referred to as the *developmental rush* as the fourth macro NIC. An underlying assumption holds that households should finance an *indirect tax state* that can use these taxes for infrastructural investments, ensuring cost efficiencies for the private sector through a supply-side strategy and financing arising from income gaps for state budgets, thereby enforcing rapid economic growth. In doing this, the state avoided increasing corporate taxes, roughly half of the OECD average, so as not to increase already high unregistered sector and employment rates (27 percent and 36 percent in 2014, respectively). The proportion of corporate taxes, taxes on income and profits, and taxes on goods and services in Turkey to the OECD average for 1965–2012 is 46 percent, 44 percent, and 74 percent, respectively (OECD 2015d).

To not risk the so-called competitive power of enterprises on the basis of low-waged labor, the state has restricted rights to organize and strike through the enactment of authoritarian labor laws, strike postponement, subcontracting, and flexible working patterns. In addition, private enterprises have exploited this opportunity to inculcate exclusive corporate governance and a wage restraint regime. Thus, the gap between labor productivity and real wages has continued to rise exponentially particularly from the early 1980s onward. Rather than mitigating consequent high income inequality through a high-quality education system as a basic means of approaching this issue (Duygan and Güner 2004), Turkish governments have perpetuated this status quo and have always organized education systems through ideological regulations. Instead, to maintain political order and economic austerity, the Turkish state has always developed patrimonial or palliative social policy strategies such as cash and in-kind social aids throughout the twentieth century. As a result, the country presented the second highest level of income inequality (0.41) after Chile and Mexico on average from 2004 to 2012. The OECD average for the same period is 0.31. Furthermore, the country's GDP per capita, 11,000 dollars by Purchasing Power Parity (PPP) as an average for 1970–2014, is much lower than the OECD average of 26,812 dollars (OECD 2015e).

Actors' fragmented identities and lack of self-reinforcing rationality along with the noninclusive regime of development combine into an *institutional trap* as the fifth macro NIC of the Turkish context. As the ultimate outcome of the country's lack of systemic governance in governing evolutionary dialectics of the NICs and PICs of its institutional stock, institutional trap in Turkish context makes sense with a NICs-dominated developmental structure consisting of such structural imperfections as comparatively lower rates of economic growth; dependence on foreign savings and intermediate goods; high current account deficits; inadequate industrial sophistication; inadequate qualified labor force stock; limited credibility between states, markets, and employees; and so on.

What caused the genesis and embedding of this trap has been the system-wide institutional fragmentation and drift at least over the last six decades, shown in Table 4.8. For example, despite the presence of strong commercial and financial deregulation, the country still presents much higher levels of product market regulation (2.8) than the OECD on average (1.7). In the same vein, employment rigidity in Turkey (2.35) is higher than the OECD average (2.17) for 1995–2013 (OECD 2015d). Turkish governments have avoided abolishing rights to severance payments to prevent taking potential political risks while also enacting flexible working patterns to reduce unemployment levels in the short run. This creates a dichotomy of *flexible rigidity* in labor supply and demand, a major cause of ongoing high levels of informal and structural unemployment under the grip of jobless growth. Such a fragmented socioeconomic strategy does not allow private employers to increase labor productivity and quality levels by imposing insecure jobs, low wages, and indecent working conditions or by developing industrial democracy, by paying decent wages, or by providing secure jobs. Instead, a dichotomous strategy between these two options has dragged the country into an institutional trap between models of productivity restraint, high unemployment, and high income inequality.

PICs in Turkish Developmental Governance

From the 1920s onward, Turkey has employed etatist liberal (1923–1929) and liberal etatist (1933–1949) models, inward and outward import-substitutionist models (1950–1959 and 1960–1979, respectively), and export-led strategies of economic development (1980–2002) along with an austerity-contingent growth model (2002 onward). As noted above, the result has been a failure to narrow the country's developmental gap with those of developed countries. In this context, emerging requirements of enforcing structural transformations from efficiency- to innovation-driven economies have led to the genesis of a new alternative: a new self-reinforcing rationale of development as the first PICs initiated by incumbent AKP governments of 2003–2015. The AKP's intermittent time in power since October of 2002 has *relatively* legitimized this rationale by mitigating negative externalities of politico-bureaucratic polarization.

Further reinforcing this initiative has been ongoing institutional, albeit not structural, improvements ranging from a consolidated macroeconomic structure and shrinking informal sector to the rising power of competition from 59 in 2006–2007 to 45 in 2014–2015 and to the improvement of business environments from 93 in 2006 to 55 in 2015 according to the GCI and Doing Business Environment Index (DBE), respectively (WEF 2006, 2015; World Bank 2006, 2015b). The country's macroeconomic structure was consolidated in terms of diminishing public sector indebtedness, ongoing financial discipline, and relatively strong banking and financial systems. Underlying the country's growing power over global competition according to the GCI has been improvements to the quality of overall infrastructures for investment, property rights, bank credit access, the increasing availability of venture capital, the effectiveness of anti-monopoly policies, hiring and firing practices, and flexibility and wage determination at various levels. These factors are suggested to be essential for achieving stable growth and for minimizing adverse effects of exogenous shocks.

The rising self-reinforcing rationale has paved the way for AKP governments to undertake or intensify their *entrepreneurial role* as a second PIC in achieving the above-noted industrial transformations. (The Turkish state's entrepreneurialism does not aim to increase the public sector's weight but rather unleash an entrepreneurial and innovative niche of economic progress. In the early 1980s, the weight of the public sector in the economy reduced significantly. The 46 state-owned enterprises that employed 635,247 civil servants and workers in 1985 were reduced to 18 in 2014, employing only 123,600 people. While the borrowing requirements of these state-owned enterprises, measured by the difference between gross investment outlays and the available resources [Celasun and Arslan 2001: 237], were 1.4 of GDP on average between 1985 and 2002, showing a fiscal deficit, it fell to −0.3 percent, showing fiscal surplus, between 2003 and 2014 [TKB 2015c: 169–170]. In parallel, public sector investment in the manufacturing sector plummeted to 0.7 of total public gross fixed investment in 2011 from 26.3 in 1980. However, this rate increased to 0.9 in 2014). In view of the persistent current account deficit, increasing private sector indebtedness, and plummeting capital productivity, the Turkish state has for the first time since the early 1980s moved beyond the Washington consensus through this initiative. In doing so, it has launched an intercomplementary, if not systemic, attempt to ensure the overall success of the country's developmental endeavors beyond a shallow redistributive or public downsizing rationale. Three main attempts made by the Turkish state, inter alia, can be suggested to best exemplify its emerging or growing entrepreneurial discretion.

The first pertains to attempts to produce a local brand of electrical cars by the Turkish Research Agency, an affiliated institution of the Turkish Ministry of Science, Technology, and Industry. In doing so, the country bought the intellectual property rights of Saab 9–3 and aims to produce a local brand in collaboration with Saab by 2020 that runs mainly on electrical battery power with a hybrid function. This initiative is in fact a direct response to the Turkish private sector's abstention in constructing a local brand automobile. Importation levels of the sector in proportion to the total manufacturing industry amounted to 8.4 percent from 1996 to 2014 on average, and the share of intermediate goods in total manufacturing was 5.6 percent for the same period, representing 63.3 percent of total imports for the automotive industry. In parallel, firms in this sector have been motivated to use import goods mainly due to the inadequacy of domestic production, due to the more qualified and uninterrupted provision of goods, and due to relationships with other firms for which Turkish firms act as a local assembly line at rates of 44, 22, and 19 percent, respectively (Saygılı et al. 2010: 86).

A second attempt has involved the development of a defense industry by the Undersecretariat for Defence Industries (SSM) in the country. The SSM is responsible for regulating the sector by planning supply-demand conditions and organizing R&D activities in developing new technologies in coordination with the private sector. From 1985 to 1990, the defense industry in Turkey imported 98 percent of its equipment from abroad. In 2011, this rate reached 12 percent (local-foreign partnerships and local firms produced 54 percent and 33 percent, respectively, of this amount). The composition of defense industry exports in 2011 consisted inter alia electronic equipment (high-tech) (27 percent), sea vehicles (13 percent), land platforms (12 percent), and air platforms (18 percent). Public and private sector firms produced 62 percent and 38 percent of this production, respectively (TOBB 2011; SSM 2014).

The Undersecretariat implemented a cluster forming strategy between subindustry firms and universities, provided R&D support and tax incentives to prioritized areas, determined quality standards, and tested purchased products. The mainstay of this industrial policy was an offset strategy that required foreign contractors to contribute to the sector's transformation by paying back a certain percentage of their pecuniary obligations by way of technology or skill transfer and investment (TKB 2014a: 44). For example, in 2009, in total offset realizations, the share of defense industry service and goods exports reached 64 percent for technological cooperation; 9 percent for investment, R&D, and education; and 5 percent for industrial participation (TOBB 2011: 56). In addition, the Undersecretariat launched a training system for its employees that involved orientation, occupational development programs for foreign language education, and funding provisions for master's programs abroad. In parallel, for sector firms, 7–10 percent of their total yearly revenues are spent on R&D. Overall, although import dependence continues for some critical equipment, the sector has a progressive and innovative vision to reduce this dependence while upgrading its technological infrastructure.

A third point relates to the operational success of Turkish Airlines (THY), which was founded as a public company in 1933. Until 2003, all scheduled domestic transport was managed under the THY's monopoly. Other private airline companies operated only in the absence of THY flights to a certain point. In 2003, this restriction was lifted. At present, 51 percent of the THY's shares has been gradually corporatized, and the remaining 49 percent is managed by the Privatization Authority. Seven of the nine members of the THY's executive board are assigned by the government, denoting that its basic policy strategies are determined by the state itself (THY 2015: 5). In stark contrast to neoclassical theories of public economics, the company increased its number of aircrafts and total flights and cargo traffic levels at a rate of 114, 152, and 131 percent from 2003 to 2011. In adapting modern management techniques quite effectively, it was ranked Europe's best airline and the World's Best Premium Economy Class Airline Seat for three consecutive years from 2011 to 2013 and retained the former title in both 2014 and 2015 (Hartigh and Küçükönal 2012).

During this process, the THY transitioned from industrial homogeneity and volume efficiency to industrial heterogeneity and efficiency allied with differentiation. In turn, the company started selling ticket online, adopted the IT infrastructure of the Miles & Smiles customer loyalty program in 2003, started applying disparate pricing on the basis of demand in 2006 and deepened this strategy in 2007 to respond to the pricing of competitors, became a full member of Star Alliance in 2008, and established the Turkish Do & Co joint venture with the Austrian firm Do & Co. In 2009, a mobile sales channel that enabled passengers to perform all procedures from their mobile phones was opened, and Turkish Airlines Technic established the Turkish Engine Center jointly with Pratt & Wittney both to transfer know-how and technology and to improve its technical service portfolio. Subsequently, the THY became a European airline with a four-star Skytrax ranking. Throughout this process, the company concentrated not only on volume but also on process efficiency. Its increasing incomes were invested in growing its scale, extending its fleet and routes, offering aggressive marketing campaigns and promotional fares, and closing and combining destinations.

The rising self-reinforcing rationality and entrepreneurial state paradigm have recently encouraged the AKP government to develop an industrial transformation program: Priority Transformation Programs (PTPs), whose constituencies are intended to be intercomplementary, as

Table 4.9 Main policy strategies of the Priority Transformation Programs

Objective	Policy strategy
Enhancing the foundation of common workplaces and industry interaction network for enterprises to develop common products and to share data and information on R&D, marketing, and so on	The formation of a database for managing supply inventory and reducing information asymmetries among national firms to increase the use of domestic inputs
Developing a model for offset practices in public procurement from abroad and promoting domestic production in high-tech areas through the ensurance of public guarantees	Development of a model for long-term collective public procurement and the establishment of the Electronic Public Procurement Platform for managing this process in order to prioritize local firms in the sectors in a structural need for technology development and domestic input
Enhancing the foundation of training centers in private sector firms to increase the relationship between theoretical and applied education through the specification of program contents in cooperation with educators and workplace managers	Canalizing the savings to financial markets through the diversification of corporate tax for the firms listed in stock market and increasing the share of commercial credits in total credits via cost differentiation and other incentives
The formation of an export and political risk insurance at certain limits for the firms to enter risky markets	

TKB (2015a)

a third PIC. The PTPs were launched as an integral part of the Tenth Development Plan of 2014–2018 to manage the country's transition from low and lower-middle-technology sectors to upper-middle and high-technology ones. The PTP's main policy strategies, inter alia, are shown in Table 4.9. On one hand, they cannot be designated as breakthroughs, as similar programs have been extensively implemented in other parts of the world. However, for Turkey, this has represented a significant break from earlier plans where each institution such as the governance of development policies or the institutionalization of SMEs had been delineated separately without systematic reference to other institutions such as information asymmetries and business clustering, respectively, whereby the former should otherwise be structured from an intercomplementary perspective.

Furthermore, unlike the one-step model of governance of the previous five-year plans, the PTPs are planned to be implemented through a process-based governance model, albeit still under a state-dominated structure. The Committee for Monitoring and Steering the Development Plan (CMSDP) is responsible for coordinating the PTPs and is managed by the high-ranking staff of relevant ministries and by the TKB's Undersecretariat, who serves as the chairman. Six-month reports are projected to be prepared by the coordinator ministry in alliance with other stakeholders and to then be delivered to the TKB. The TKB will be held responsible for the Board of Ministers, and this responsibility will be mediated by the CMSDP. The data will be transferred to the action monitoring system for use by all stakeholders.

The reformation of the country's incentive system in 2012 can also be suggested to have served as a complementary presage for PTPs as well. The reform aimed to encourage the private sector to invest in high-tech sectors to reduce inter-regional differences and current account deficits. This involves subsidizing efficiency-enhancing inputs such as the pharmaceutical and defense industry, education, tourism, and transportation; the strategic prioritization of investment goods and products (more than 50 percent of which are produced through import goods); the selective subsidization of high-tech and innovative investments; the further enhancement of investments to be made through sectorial collaboration and in organized industrial zones; and so on (TEB 2015).

4.7   Explaining the Institutional Trap of G&D in Turkey

With its entrenched NICs and a number of emerging PICs, Turkish developmental structure does not have a systemic governance regime for managing evolutionary complications of these NICs and PICs. The question that thus arises concerns whether systemic governance drawn upon these emerging PICs could be possible in the Turkish context.

The most significant change in the country's developmental PICs has been the state's nascent entrepreneurial initiatives in leading industrial and operational sophistication. Such an initiative has been accompanied by a thriving capacity for self-reinforcing rationality and by a growing rationale of cross-institutional, albeit nonsystemic, transformation. On one hand, such an entrepreneurial initiative presents transformational potential, as it represents the inception of de-accumulation in pursuing developmental strategies on the basis of institutional fragmentation and drift. The THY's success in international competition and the SSM's relative success in leading the production of high-tech products in cooperation with the private sector show that the Turkish state could lead in overall industrial sophistication as well if it extends a kindred strategic governance policy to other industrial areas. Some outstanding projects such as the Third Bridge and Third Airport (the largest of their type in the world) in Istanbul that are being conducted via public-private partnerships (TKB 2014e: 53–58) also serve as strong indicators in this respect. Furthermore, the PTPs and growing institutional capacities would reinforce this entrepreneurial initiative in systemic terms.

On the other hand, the PICs present limited capacities to spur systemic transformation. Underlying this are three main factors. The first relates to the fact that the five major NICs shown in Table 4.8 represent both systemic and path-dependent dynamics dating back to the first half of the nineteenth century that they become embedded in dialectics with overall politico-economic cultures. However, the three nascent PICs have been a matter of the last decade or so, and their impact has been partial rather than systemic. A culture of systemic governance in a PICs-dominated direction can be forged through inter-reinforcing dialectics of overall politico-economic and informal institutions but not only through institutional design per se. In this sense, in Turkey, an enduring culture of nonsystemic developmental governance and institutional drift under the grasp of actors' diffused identities constitutes the most formidable challenge in the face of transitions to systemic governance in time.

The PTPs, established in early 2014, did not touch (even tangentially) on an inclusive model of governance either. Prior to the general elections of October of 2015, the incumbent AKP pledged to increase minimum wage by roughly 30 percent without negotiating with business or worker organizations. This increase, which covers roughly five million minimum-waged workers (28 percent of all workers employed in the manufacturing sector), served as the first significant test to determine whether the PTPs could be enforced from a systemic governance perspective, as it will cause a 20 percent increase in manufacturing firm production costs. Thus, ex post, process-based governance mechanisms of the PTPs in theory cannot be claimed to fundamentally overwhelm another systemic NIC, the overautonomous state, in praxis under current structures of economic governance.

No less important than the previous two, the third point relates to the fact that the performance of the Turkish private sector with its stock of enterprises, banks, and labor force over the past five decades is not as robust in carrying out the private aims of a self-reinforcing development strategy and of the PTPs. There are mainly three issues that would restrict the feasibility of such a positive dynamic. The first pertains to the fact that Turkish private sector firms have adapted themselves to imports but not to the production of high-tech intermediate goods (at least over the past five decades), and there is no workable public governance mechanism to be orchestrated by reformist bureaucratic strata for the development of an innovative culture. The second pertains to the fact that there is no established on-the-job training system between firms and labor organizations or between firms themselves and there is no planned systemic transformation (despite the existence of some ad hoc initiatives) in the higher education system that can train enough qualified technical laborers for employment in prospective high-tech sectors. Third, it would be too optimistic in view of Turkish banking sector performance particularly over the past two decades to suggest that this would provide long-term financing for risky entrepreneurial projects to be conducted under harsh levels of international competition.

In the end, it seems difficult (if not impossible) to suggest that emerging reform dynamics could unleash a PICs-dominated systemic governance regime in Turkey that could harness systemic and micro NICs, and particularly institutional fragmentation and drift and its negative externalities of limited industrial sophistication; dependence on imported intermediate goods; limited credible commitment between the state, market, and society; and high income inequality. The underlying factors of these imperfections are in their place to a great extent, and the so-called dynamics aim to spur a sharp transformation through a central institutional design. The Turkish state does not wield authoritarian systemic governance capacities to impel the private sector to adopt an innovative and export-led strategy, nor does it intend to embark on a (democratic) systemic governance strategy to manage the evolutionary complications of NICs and PICs with the private sector to achieve economic efficiency, industrial sophistication, and social equity. Instead, the PTPs have been drafted without consideration of the evolutionary complications of the (macro-micro) NICs and PICs.

The first two-year outcomes of the Tenth Development Plan for 2014–2018 provide some clues in this sense. As shown in Table 4.10, the Medium-Term Plan for 2016–2018 revised the Tenth Development Plan's targeted growth rate, total domestic savings, and unemployment levels from 5.5 percent, 19 percent, and 8.2 percent for 2014–2018 to 3.8 percent, 17.2 percent, and 9.9 percent, respectively, for 2016–2018. Other factors that prevent us from making positive predictions relate to the fact that the TKB aims to keep the value added of industry to GDP at the same level of approximately 20 percent as an average for 2014–2018 to increase the manufacturing value added by only approximately 6.4 percent from 15.5 percent in 2013, increasing the share of medium-high-technology products at a rate of 2 percent from 31 percent in 2013.

Table 4.10 Macroeconomic projections of Turkish economy, 2014–2018

	Five-year plan—target for		Medium-term plan target for
Parameters	2018	2014–2018 (average)	2016–2018
Growth (%)	5.9	5.5	3.88
TFP (in industry)	1.2	1.1	–
Industry (value added to GDP, %)	20.4	19.9	–
Manufacturing (value added to GDP, %)	16.5	–	–
Unemployment rate (%)	7.2	8.2	9.9
Share of mid-high-tech	32.1	–	–

Source: TKB (2014b, 2015b)

Overall, the institutional trap into which Turkey has fallen in particular over the last one decade is continuing with its all trappings. At present, the country is unable to turn its NICs-dominated G&D structure into a PICs-dominated one, because the policymakers have been stuck between the rush to create structural changes for getting political popularity and the path dependencies of a NICs-dominated structure in an enduring fragmentation and drift.

4.8   Conclusion

The Turkish case illustrates that the systemic governance of complementarities serves as the essential precondition in preventing the genesis and embedding of institutional fragmentation that is bound to result in a process of developmental drift as a main cause of structural imperfections. Rather than pursuing systemic governance, the country has predicated its development strategies either on transposed ideas or reactive restructuration. These *strategies* have been adapted not to manage the evolutionary and idiosyncratic complications of the country's NICs and PICs to achieve overarching and long-term developmental objectives but as a bureaucratic framework for implementing the faltering policy strategies of short-lived governments. In a period when the country's institutional stock has become stuck in institutional trap, the incumbent AKP government has started to transform the country's dependent institutional and industrial structures by launching an entrepreneurial state paradigm and by focusing on (prioritizing) industrial transformation programs (PTPs).

Whereas such a strategic initiative would be critical to realizing a complementarity-oriented transformation, it has failed to a great extent due to the ignorance of the country's path-dependent NICs from a systemic perspective. The institutional drift of the country's developmental institutions has not only caused the genesis of structural imperfections ranging from comparatively lower economic growth to high structural unemployment but has also constrained the construction of such a strategic reform initiative because these imperfections have come to dominate the systemic functioning of Turkish developmental regime. An exhaustive analysis of how such systemic governance should be adopted in the Turkish context and of what types of institutional changes are required (major questions in themselves) should apparently be the subject matter of further research.

References

Altuğ, S., Filiztekin, A., & Pamuk, Ş. (2008). Sources of Long-Term Growth for Turkey, 1880–2005. *European Review of Economic History, 12*(3), 393–430.

Ararat, M. (2011). Comply or Explain Without Consequences: The Case of Turkey. In C. A. Mallin (Ed.), *Handbook on International Corporate Governance* (pp. 355–370). Cheltenham: Edward Elgar.

Bakır, C., & Öniş, Z. (2010). The Regulatory State and Turkish Banking Reforms in the Age of Post-Washington Consensus. *Development and Change, 41*(1), 77–106.

Banking Regulation and Supervision Agency (BDDK). (2014). *Türk Bankacılık Sektörü Temel Göstergeleri*. Aralık, Ankara.

Bayar, A. H. (1996). The Developmental State and Economic Policy in Turkey. *Third World Quarterly, 17*(4), 773–785.

Berkes, N. (1964). *The Development of Secularism in Turkey*. Montreal: McGill University Press.

Biddle, J., & Minor, V. (1997). Economic Governance in Turkey: Bureaucratic Capacity, Policy Networks, and Business Associations. In S. Maxfield & B. R. Schneider (Eds.), *Business and the State in Developing Countries* (pp. 277–310). Ithaca: Cornell University Press.

Boratav, K., Türel, O., & Yeldan, E. (1996). Dilemmas of Structural Adjustment and Environmental Policies Under Stability: Post-1980 Turkey. *World Development, 24*(2), 373–393.

Celasun, M., & Arslan, I. (2001). State-Owned Enterprises and Privatization in Turkey. In M. Celasun (Ed.), *State-Owned Enterprises in the Middle East and North Africa* (pp. 224–252). London: Routledge.

Central Bank of Turkey (TCMB). (2002). *The Impact of Globalization on Turkish Economy*. Ankara: TCMB.

Çiller, T. (1972). *The Strategy of Economic Development: The Turkish Case*. PhD Dissertation, University of Connecticut, Connecticut.

Duygan, B., & Güner, N. (2004). Income and Consumption Inequality in Turkey: What Role Does Education Play? In S. Altuğ & A. Filiztekin (Eds.),

The Turkish Economy: The Real Economy, Corporate Governance and Reform (pp. 63–91). London: Routledge.

Eser, E. (2011). *Türkiye'de Uygulanan Yatırım Teşvik Sistemleri ve Mevcut Sistemin Yapısına Yönelik Öneriler.* Ankara: İktisadi Sektörler ve Koordinasyon Genel Müdürlüğü.

Hartigh, E. D., & Küçükönal, H. (2012). The Turkish Aviation System and the Strategy of Turkish Airlines. In R. Curran (Ed.), *Air Transport and Operations* (pp. 231–246). Amsterdam: IOS Press.

Karpat, K. (2004). *Studies in Turkish Politics and Society.* Leiden: Brill.

Kepenek, Y. (2008). *Türkiye Ekonomisi.* İstanbul: Remzi.

NTV. (2015). *Yargı Bağımsızlığı.* Retrieved March 4, 2015, from http://arsiv.ntv.com.tr/ntv/metinler/neden/20071211.asp

OECD. (2014). *OECD Economic Surveys: Turkey 2014.* Paris: OECD.

OECD. (2015a). *OECD STAN Statistics.* Retrieved October 8, 2015, from http://stats.oecd.org/Index.aspx?DataSetCode=STANI4#

OECD. (2015b). *Mathematics Performance (PISA).* Retrieved October 4, 2015, from https://data.oecd.org/pisa/mathematics-performance-pisa.htm

OECD. (2015c). *Science Performance (PISA).* Retrieved October 4, 2015, from https://data.oecd.org/pisa/science-performance-pisa.htm#indicator-chart

OECD. (2015d). *Public Sector, Taxation and Market Regulation Statistics.* Retrieved October 6, 2015, from http://stats.oecd.org/

OECD. (2015e). *National Accounts Statistics.* Retrieved October 6, 2015, from http://stats.oecd.org/

Öniş, Z. (1998). *State and Market: The Political Economy of Turkey in Comparative Perspective.* İstanbul: Bosphorus University Press.

Saygılı, Ş., Cihan, C., Yalçın, C., & Hamsici, T. (2010). *Türkiye İmalat Sanayinin İthalat Yapısı.* TCMB Working Papers 2010/2. Retrieved December 8, 2015, from http://www.tcmb.gov.tr/wps/wcm/connect/8b16265d-2fcb-4ce3-944b-dd2cfb967750/WP1002.pdf?MOD=AJPERES&CACHEID=ROOTWORKSPACE8b16265d-2fcb-4ce3-944b-dd2cfb967750

Steinherr, A., Tukel, A., & Ucer, M. (2004, August). *The Turkish Banking Sector: Challenges and Outlook in Transition to the EU Membership.* EU-Turkey Working Papers, Centre for European Policy Studies. Retrieved September 8, 2015, from http://aei.pitt.edu/6762/

The Undersecretariat of Defence Ministry (SSM). (2014). *Faaliyet Raporu.* Ankara: SSM.

THY. (2015). *Türk Hava Yolları Anonim Ortaklığı Ana Sözleşmesi.* Retrieved October 19, 2015, from http://www.turkishairlines.com/download/investor_relations/kurumsal_yonetim/AnaSozlesme_Turkce.pdf

TKB. (2000). *Kamu Yönetiminin İyileştirilmesi ve Yeniden Yapılandırılması Özel İhtisas Komisyonu Raporu.* Ankara: TKB.

TKB. (2007). *Kamu'da İyi Yönetişim.* Ankara: TKB.

TKB. (2014a). *Kamu Yönetimi Özel İhtisas Komisyonu Raporu.* Ankara: TKB.

TKB. (2014b). *10th Development Plan.* Ankara: TKB.

TKB. (2014c). *2014–2018 Stratejik Plan.* Ankara: TKB.

TKB. (2014d). *İmalat Sanayinde Dönüşüm Özel İhtisas Komisyonu Raporu.* Ankara: TKB.

TKB. (2014e). *Kamu Özel İşbirliği Özel İhtisas Komisyonu Raporu.* Ankara: TKB.

TKB. (2015a). *Öncelikli Dönüşüm Programları.* Retrieved June 27, 2015, from http://odop.kalkinma.gov.tr/

TKB. (2015b). *2016–2018 Orta Vadeli Program.* Retrieved July 14, 2015, from http://www.kalkinma.gov.tr/Pages/OrtaVadeliProgramlar.aspx

TKB. (2015c). *Ekonomik ve Sosyal Göstergeler.* Retrieved July 16, 2015, from http://www.kalkinma.gov.tr/Pages/EkonomikSosyalGostergeler.aspx

Turkish Chambers of Commerce (TOBB). (2011). *Türkiye Savunma Sanayi Sektör Raporu.* Ankara: TOBB.

Turkish Ministry of Economy (TEB). (2015). *Yatırım Teşvik Bülteni—Temmuz 2015.* Ankara: TEB.

Turkish Statistical Institution (TSI). (2013). *İstatistik Göstergeler, 1923–2011.* Ankara: TSI.

Uçkan, B. (2013). Two Steps Forward, One Step Back, or Vice Versa: The New Legal Framework of Collective Labour Relations in Turkey. *Transfer: European Review of Labor and Research, 19*(4), 569–579.

Ugur, M., & Ararat, M. (2006). Macroeconomic Instability and Corporate Governance Quality in Turkey: Scope for Optimism. *Corporate Governance, 14*(4), 325–348.

Wade, R. (1990). *Governing the Market.* Princeton: Princeton University Press.

World Bank. (2006). *Doing Business Report 2006: Creating Jobs.* Washington, DC: World Bank.

World Bank. (2015a). *World Development Indicators.* Retrieved October 4, 2015, from http://databank.worldbank.org/data/reports.aspx?source=world-development-indicators

World Bank. (2015b). *Doing Business Report 2015: Going Beyond Efficiency.* Washington, DC: World Bank.

World Economic Forum (WEF). (2006). *Global Competitiveness Report 2006–2007.* Geneva: WEF.

World Economic Forum (WEF). (2015). *Global Competitiveness Report 2006–2007*. Geneva: WEF.

Yavan, N. (2011). *Teşviklerin Sektörel ve Bölgesel Analizi: Türkiye Örneği*. Ankara: Maliye Hesap Uzmanları Vakfı Yayınları.

Index

© The Author(s) 2018
T. Akan, *The Complementary Roots of Growth and Development*,
https://doi.org/10.1007/978-3-319-68932-6

Printed by Books on Demand, Germany